AN UNSELFISH
A BOMBER CRE

★★★★★★★★★★★★★★★

DEADLY
DECISION

RICK CENTORE

ISBN: 1-4392-6367-1
EAN13: 9781439263679
Library of Congress Control Number: 2009911171

This book is dedicated to the Gold Star Kids
of the 492nd Bomb Group

Kathy Nursall Jensen

Billy Sheely Johnson

Judith Larivee O'Connor

Patrick Byrne

TABLE OF CONTENTS

ACKNOWLEDGEMENTS

Without the help of family and friends, this book could not have been written. My stepmother, Jean Centore, encouraged Dad to write his personal history for his family. When he did put pen to paper he was eighty years old. He could have written about any part of that long life. He chose to expound on the four years he spent in the service of his country. That fact alone speaks volumes on the importance he placed on those experiences.

My very patient wife Lynne put up with my obsession to see this process through. She was my sounding board and brought forward many valuable ideas and insights. Lynne accompanied me to many reunions of the 492nd Bomb Group. We made many new friends in the process.

Several people read early drafts of the book. They were asked to note mistakes in grammar, spelling, or punctuation. They were also asked to point out passages that were not clear. Their efforts helped me immeasurably and I very appreciative.

My son Mike works in the publishing field in New York City. He edited this work, not only on my behalf, but because he sees this work as a tribute to his grandfather.

My friend George Hathaway, who I have known since we were teenagers, is himself a published author. His enthusiasm, encouragement, and knowledge kept me focused on bringing this project to fruition.

My friend and neighbor, Phil DePietro, took time from his busy schedule to do a very thorough reading of this book. He made numerous suggestions and constructive criticisms. In the end, every one of them was taken and adopted.

My sister, Judy Stephens, employed her long experience as a secretary to insure that the narrative was properly written. She and my brothers, Chip and Tom, scoured their memories for stories Dad had told them over the years. Their recollections helped immensely and all are included.

My niece, Jen Stephens, utilized her extensive knowledge of computer graphics on the cover design. Her grandfather would be very proud of her efforts.

The website 492ndbombgroup.com is a collaborative effort of brothers Paul & Dave Arnett. It was an invaluable resource in researching this book. There are many sites dedicated to military units but this is hands down the best on the web.

• • •

INTRODUCTION

The Eighth Air Force of World War II has been immortalized in numerous books and films. From 1942 to the defeat of Germany in 1945 its 48 Bomb Groups (BG) pummeled strategic targets in Hitler's Third Reich. At its peak in the summer of 1944, it was staffed by over 200,000 officers and enlisted men and women. Over the course of the war, 350,000 served in its ranks. Twenty-six thousand of its members were killed in action (KIA), while twenty thousand others were captured and spent the remainder of the war as prisoners of war (POW).

The 492nd Bomb Group has the unenviable distinction of being the only bomb group to be disbanded due to excessive losses. In 89 days, from May 11, 1944, to August 7, 1944, the 492nd flew 66 combat missions and lost 55 aircraft. Crew 601 was one of them. On June 20, 1944 their aircraft was shot down in flames, four men were dead, and the survivors were marched off to a German prison camp.

My father, Technical Sergeant Nello Centore, was the flight engineer on Crew 601. The time he spent in the military, and especially his experience as a prisoner of war, had a profound impact on him. We prodded him to write about his experiences and he finally did. This book was originally based on a journal Dad wrote in 2000. He gave it to me the following year and I put it aside knowing that I would one day transcribe it. We moved in 2001 and 2007 and the diary got packed away. Every so often I would look for it unsuccessfully and feared it might have been lost forever. Dad passed away on October 11, 2007. In February, 2008 I discovered the unmarked green wire-wound notebook in the bottom of a bookcase. The journal is 50 handwritten pages long. It is not a diary of his time in the service as it was written from memory over 50 years after the events. While going through his personal effects in 2009 I found more of his writings. He had also saved my Mother's letters to him and an essay written by her for a college course.

After I completed transcribing the journals, my curiosity was aroused. I wanted to find out more. Were his recollections correct? What was happening to other crews and individuals? I began my research. My original objective was simply to document family history. But after sharing the story, I was told by others it was a compelling one. The lesson of Deadly Decision is that the choices we make, although they may seem minor at the time, can have totally unexpected repercussions.

The journals were broken into chapters. After each chapter I have added a commentary. I did this for clarity and to put my Dad's remembrances into a larger context. The information in the commentaries was gleaned from conversations I had with Dad and other veterans, miscellaneous publications, and Internet research. Chapters have been inserted to aid the reader in understanding terminology and subsequent events. To differentiate between my words and those of my parents, their words are in italics.

I have also integrated my Mother's writings into the narrative. She is also a hero of this story. On June, 20, 1944 she was nineteen years old and six months pregnant. It was then that she received the news; Dad was MIA, missing in action. It would be two more months before she found out that he was alive. She died in an auto accident in 1975. At that time I was a self-absorbed 30 year-old and never fully appreciated the anguish she must have suffered. I do now.

It is my hope that the reader will come away with an appreciation for the sacrifices of the men of the 492nd Bomb Group, the hard luck outfit of the Eighth Air Force.

• • •

CHAPTER 1
THE EARLY YEARS

Nello B. Centore was born in Beloit, Wisconsin on December 12, 1919. He was the son of immigrants. His mother, Louisa Debegnach, was born in 1898 in Udine, Italy. In 1916 she married Giuseppe Sturnick. They had two sons. George was born in 1918 and Nello in 1919. Louisa's relationship with Giuseppe was bitter and ended in divorce. No pictures of him exist and information is minimal. In 1927 she married 37 year old Angelo Centore. He was a veteran of the Alpini, the Italian Army's mountain troops. Much of the family's early days are shrouded in mystery. The family owned a boarding house in Milwaukee, Wisconsin. They may have lost it after the Crash of 1929. After that they left Wisconsin and moved to Albany, New York. In 1930 they took the night steamboat down the Hudson River and moved to New York City. Louisa and Angelo worked at Bellevue Hospital, a short walk from their apartment on East 34th Street. George also served in World War II. He was a member of the combat engineers and served in North Africa, Sicily, Italy, and France. Although Angelo never adopted George and Nello, in 1940 the boys had their names legally changed to Centore.

The 1930s have been called the "Golden Age of Aviation." Flyers were the astronauts of their day. Nello was caught up in the latest technology and built airplane models at the kitchen table and flew them in the park. He attended high school at New York City's School of Aviation Trades. After graduation in 1937 he could not find a job in his chosen field. He blamed his lack of employment in aviation on the fact that at 18 years old he was only four feet and 10 inches tall and looked like a kid. He found work at the Torrington Company in Torrington, Connecticut, as a bearing inspector. He boarded with Gino Soliani and his family. Between 1937 and his enlistment in 1942 he added nine inches to his height and entered the Army at a respectable five foot seven.

• • •

The Centore family in 1929. (L-R) Nello, Louisa, Angelo, George (Author)

CHAPTER 2
YOU'RE IN THE ARMY NOW!

In September of 1941 I received my draft notice, but I wasn't prepared to become a ground pounder (infantry man). I created a hardship story to give the Draft Board. At the hearing they tried many ways to break my story. Mr. Smith, the head of the Draft Board, was also my boss at the Torrington Company in Torrington, Connecticut. In the end I was awarded a six-month deferment. When Pearl Harbor happened I was in a pickle because we were now at war with Japan and Germany. Now I had to undo my story so I could volunteer. Between September and December I was exploring ways I could slip off to Canada to join the RCAF (Royal Canadian Air Force). After Christmas I went before the Draft Board and told them the family problems (which didn't exist) were resolved and I had the blessing of my parents to proceed and enlist. I went to the Navy first. They were impressed with my trade school training and offered me a Machinist Mate 3rd Class rating upon enlistment. I passed all their requirements except dental. I didn't have enough teeth, which at that time was 32. At that time they hadn't lowered the requirement even though we were at war. I tried the Marines but they had the same requirements as the Navy. I turned to the Air Corps and passed because I could see lightning and hear thunder—and enough teeth to eat Army chow. Funny thing though, my brother-in-law Lou went into the Navy. The first thing they did was to pull his teeth and give him upper and lower plates. I had good teeth but just not enough of them.

On January 19, 1942, I was officially in the service. I took the oath in Hartford, Connecticut. That evening we all boarded the train for Fort Devens, Massachusetts. Leaving the train we walked around puddles of water, slush, and mud so we wouldn't get our shoes and suits dirty. By the end of this long day, tired and worn out, we were slogging through the muck. We would soon have no need for civilian clothes anyway. By midnight we were assigned bedding and assigned to a barracks. As I drifted off to sleep you could hear some guys, who must never have been away from home, weeping. Believe me, 5 A.M. came too soon. The lights turned on and the Drill Instructors started yelling for us to get up, shave, shower, and get dressed. Breakfast was in one hour. Somehow we made it. It was a busy day. Uniforms were issued, shots were given, and we ran around the base for all sorts of orientation classes.

I checked the assignment board and found myself on mess duty from 6 P.M. to 8 A.M. the next morning. Being the last guy there I was assigned to pots and pans—and the evening meal was macaroni and cheese. When everyone else was finished with their jobs I was still scrubbing and chiseling dried macaroni and cheese from countless pans to the satisfaction of the Mess Sergeant. He was an alcoholic who drank lemon extract for its high alcohol content. I made it through the night and while everyone was leaving the barracks I was just walking in to get some sleep. They returned around noon and the commotion woke me up. So I shaved, showered, and went to lunch with them. That afternoon we took a five-mile hike. I found out later that my overnight duties entitled me to the day off, but too late to do me any good.

After Fort Devens we were to go to Keesler, Florida, for basic training but an outbreak of meningitis there meant a change of orders to Fort Dix, New Jersey. (Note: The basic training base Dad is referring to was at Keesler Field in Biloxi, Mississippi.) Our scheduled eight weeks of basic training kept getting shortened until we were deemed basic soldiers after only 10 days.

I was assigned to the 57th Observation Group based right there at Fort Dix. Grabow, Shebat, and I were assigned to the flight line. All together there were 10 of us. We worked for the Line Chief, Sergeant Wetzler. One of the guys was named Collins. We were told he was an army brat and a relation of General Lawton Collins but we didn't know that for a fact. He had so many accidents while taxiing aircraft that we called him "Crash Collins." Our little group serviced the Flight Instrument School aircraft as well as refueling and maintenance of transient aircraft. One day out of the blue came 50 new Piper Cubs from the factory in Lock Haven, Pennsylvania. Now we 10 men were burdened with pre-flight inspections, daily inspections, and service for over 50 airplanes. Newly graduated pilots joined the outfit and some of them eventually became members of the 492nd Bomb Group. By the end of June, 1942, the Cubs were gone, personnel were reassigned, and the 57th was disbanded.

I was sent to the 104th Observation Squadron at Bader Field in Atlantic City, New Jersey. This was good for me because this is where I met my wife, Ethel. I was a PFC but was promoted to corporal in September. I was assigned to a crew chief named Messick. We were flying the Douglas O-46 and the North American O-47 on coastal patrol in conjunction with the Civil Air Patrol. The CAP was also based at Bader Field. An incident occurred during that summer that is worth telling. A B-17 experienced engine trouble and could not make it to Fort Dix so they opted to land at Bader Field and make repairs. After repairs were made the bomber lined up on our longest runway, ready for takeoff. The runway was less than 4,000 feet long and gravel-surfaced. The flaps were set at the take off position and the pilot held the brakes. He revved the engines to take off power and released the brakes. We figured that if he didn't have suffi-cient airspeed by the time he crossed the runway intersection he was go-ing to be in serious trouble. He raised the tail as he gained speed. When he reached the intersection it looked marginal at best. At that moment, instead of aborting the takeoff, the pilot dropped full flaps and the B-17 lumbered into the air. Luckily, he raised the landing gear just in time for the wheels to clear the trees and obstacles at the end of the runway. After some anxious moments the pilot made a 180-degree turn and returned to make a low level pass over the field. We gave him the V sign as he wagged his wings and climbed into the wild blue.

We were doing anti-submarine patrols, but in the time I was there I don't think any of our pilots spotted a sub. We stayed in Atlantic City until December of 1942. The 104th Observation Squadron was transferred to Langley Field in Virginia. In November of 1942 we became the 12th Anti-Sub Squadron. We turned in the O-46 and O-47 aircraft and began train-ing on the Douglas B-18 Bolo, the bomber version of the famous DC-2 and DC-3 series of airliners. I began this phase still on the ground crew as assistant crew chief to a regular army Technical Sergeant who was an alcoholic. In a sense I was the crew chief because he was always nursing a hangover. I don't know how he ever made Technical Sergeant in the first place. I was promoted to Sergeant but my requests for my own air-craft were ignored. The 104th was a National Guard outfit that had been federalized and they took care of their own.

The B-18 I was assigned to was always in an "up" status and was the only one with a working heating system. I went on a seven-day leave and returned only to find that the drunkard had neglected to drain the heat-ing system after a flight as I always did. One freezing night a water line ruptured and rendered the system inoperable. Captain Clark, our Main-tenance Officer, refused to give us time to repair the system. His orders were to forget about the heaters as long as the aircraft was otherwise air-worthy. I received a reprimand during this time for taxiing a B-18 across *an active runway. My third crewman was my observer. He watched the control tower for a green light as we approached the runway. He said we had the green so I went across. It turned out that a P-47 Thunderbolt was on final approach for landing. The observer denied giving me the green. Along with the reprimand I had to take refresher classes with another Sergeant before I was allowed to taxi another aircraft. Yet, I was still stuck with the two losers. When I heard they were looking for volunteers for flight engineer training I took advantage of it. Part of my motivation was to get away from the unpleasant situation I found myself in.*

COMMENTARY

In the patriotic fervor that followed the attack on Pearl Harbor, Dad was caught in the lie he told the draft board three months before. He describes the desire to join the Royal Canadian Air Force. But world events moved too quickly for that plan to have come to fruition. Many Americans did join the RCAF and the British Royal Air Force. The RAF had organized three "Eagle Squadrons" that were staffed entirely by Americans. They waged war against Nazi Germany during the Battle of Britain. In September of 1942, after the United States' entry into the war, the Eagle Squadrons were reorganized and became the American Fourth Fighter Group.

The American war effort was getting into high gear. Basic training of 10 days is hardly sufficient, but there was little choice for the War Department. The task at hand was staggering. When World War II began in September of 1939, the United States had an army of 175,000 officers and men. Four years later the number had skyrocketed to over 8 million. That is an unbelievable forty seven-fold increase. Mobilization at that scale required the entire nation to be put on a war footing. President Roosevelt declared the United States to be the "arsenal of democracy." In early 1942 automobile production ceased and public works projects were put on hold as manufacturing turned from consumer goods to weapons of war.

The 104th Observation Squadron flew the ungainly Douglas O-46, which looked like an overgrown Piper Cub, and the North American O-47. They were conceived as platforms for photographing enemy troop movements and other reconnaissance missions. Although both types were designed only in the late 1930s, by 1942 both types were deemed obsolete. They would have been "sitting ducks" if used in actual combat. But this was early in the war and aircraft production was still catching up with the needs of the Army Air Force. So they did soldier on, but were relegated to training, target towing, and—in this case—patrols off the east coast of the United States. In actual practice the most effective recon aircraft proved to be standard front line fighters equipped with cameras. They had the speed and armament to defend against enemy aircraft.

Dad was accepted for flight engineer training. He doesn't explain if he was sent to a formal school or if it was on-the-job training conducted within the 12th Anti-Sub Squadron. But he was put on flight status and thus eligible for flight pay in March of 1943. He flew for the next 16 months as a flight engineer and gunner and accumulated 560 hours total flight time.

• • •

The Douglas O-46 and the North American O-47 were deemed inadequate for combat and were relegated to stateside duties. (Ramsay Library, New England Air Museum)

CHAPTER 3
HUNTING U-BOATS

In March of 1943 I was put on flight status and began flying as a flight engineer. As such I was required to go to gunnery school at Tyndall Field, Florida. I got there two weeks early and was put into a receiving squadron to await the start of classes. Four of us were NCOs and the rest were just out of basic training at St. Petersburg, Florida. We were there for two weeks before we began training. During this time we were restricted to our barracks. We weren't supposed to go to the PX, the movies, or the NCO club. But, of course, we went there anyway. We didn't like all these restrictions being placed on us. The 2nd Lieutenant in charge of us had washed-out of West Point but apparently still liked the strict discipline of the academy. Once we started classes all restrictions were lifted. However, we were kept so busy that we seldom had time to go to the PX, the movies, or the NCO club. We had classes all day, tearing down machine guns and reassembling them blindfolded. We had pistol classes and classes on turrets. We shot trap to hone our shooting skills both standing on the ground and firing from trucks being driven through a maze where clay pigeons were fired from all directions. I wish my father had taken the time to show me more about shooting. I shot mainly marksman with one sharpshooter badge. The last two weeks were spent on air-to-air gunnery. We fired at targets towed behind another aircraft from the back seat of a North American AT-6 Texan trainer. Once proficient with the post mounted gun, we progressed to firing from the dorsal turret of a Lockheed AT-18. The AT-18 was a trainer version of the Hudson bomber.

I flew 17 patrols as flight engineer. There were two that I remember well. I was awakened one night for an emergency submarine sighting. We took off in our B-18 and headed south following the coastline. The pilot aroused the attention of every aircraft spotting station until we turned east and out to sea off the coast of North Carolina. The radar operator started calling out the number of miles to the target. I cranked the manually operated turret into position. I believe we were flying between 800 to 1,200 feet, close enough to see whitecaps. The radar operator said the target was 25 miles away, then 15, then 10, then three. Standard operating procedure was to turn on the landing lights to illuminate the target. The bombardier opened the bomb bay doors one mile from the target and called out that the target was in sight. At the last possible moment the bombardier said it was a fishing trawler. We circled the area and the radar man flashed a Morse code signal with a hand-held light. The trawler returned the proper response. With that we headed home. That afternoon we attended a briefing given by pilots from the Jacksonville, Florida-based squadron. They told us they lost aircraft to submarines that remained on the surface. When the landing lights were turned on the Germans aimed between them and shot the aircraft down. No one had informed our outfit of that. We who flew the previous night looked at each other and realized how vulnerable we had been. After that the policy for using landing lights was changed.

First Lt. Herschel Smith (492nd BG Crew 906) was our pilot on an anti-sub patrol in June or July of 1943. (Note: Flight records show this was in June; in July he flew nine hours in a North American B-25 and had no B-18 time.) While on patrol the MAD (Magnetic Anomaly Detector) on our B-18 went crazy, alerting us that something was underwater, possibly a submarine. Smith made a circular pass and told me to be ready to drop a sea marker. The marker was a bag of aluminum powder, which we called "slick." The bag would break open on impact and was quite visible from the air. I removed the small door insert from the main cabin door and grabbed a bag of slick from the storage container. I stood poised to drop on command. Smith waved his hand, and as I started to push the bag of slick out the door the bag burst. The aluminum powder aluminized me and the interior of the aft fuselage. I asked Smith to go around again. This time I used a type of slick that came in a glass container and was successful. Smitty flew ever increasing circles around the sea marker but we found no submarine. We did see three whales swimming in formation though. I was told to photograph them. However the photo shop didn't want any more aircraft wings in the pictures so I asked Smitty to bank a bit more to get a better shot. He turned the controls over to the co-pilot 2nd Lt. Lofdahl. When he banked I took the picture, but he had banked too much. The aircraft started to sideslip. I looked up to the cockpit and saw both pilots on the controls. At one point the aircraft just hung there not responding to any control input. All of a sudden Smith applied full power to the left engine (we were banked to the left) and the aircraft rolled right. I wasn't holding onto anything except the camera. I hit the right side of the fuselage. As the aircraft leveled off I hit the left side—but never dropped the camera.

When we were homeward bound the radar operator reported a message from the destroyer U.S.S. Spence. They had sunk a submarine within the convoy. We landed back at Langley Field. When I got out of the aircraft I was covered with the aluminum slick. I was called the "Silver Knight of the Skies" for a while after that. By December of 1943 anti-submarine patrols were turned over to the Navy.

The 12th Anti-Sub Squadron was transferred to Blythe, California. That's pretty good, an anti-sub outfit in the desert! We must have done a good job because no submarines appeared in Blythe while we were there. The duty was good and light. We played baseball and sat in the sun, but we froze at night. We had to travel from the furthest point on the base to reach the PX. Sometimes we walked and sometimes we hitched a ride on a truck. At the PX we watched movies, drank beer, and just hung loose.

Our Maintenance Officer brought the easy days to an end when he volunteered our line and flight crews to help the 30th or 36th Bomb Group stationed at Blythe. They were having trouble getting their aircraft to "up" status. In a very short time we had 90 percent in flying status. Of course many 2nd Air Force rules were stretched or broken to accomplish this.

This area was under the control of General Newton Longfellow. Nature had played a trick on him as he was about five foot six and not properly named. He was a stickler about rules and regulations. One of his orders was that if a sandstorm came up, all aircraft were to land, regardless of whether the pilot could make it to an alternate field or had sufficient fuel to wait it out until the storm passed. You couldn't see the runways when the sandstorm hit. The pilots flew by compass headings. Some landed short; others ran out of runway and just crashed.

COMMENTARY

Early in World War II German submarines roamed up and down the east coast of the United States. Between December of 1941 and September of 1942 they sank over 200 cargo ships and tankers, often within sight of American shores. Called U-boats from the German Unterseeboot, they were the targets of the Anti-Submarine Squadrons of the Army Air Force. The Army and Navy had clashed over who had responsibility for airborne anti-submarine warfare (ASW). In 1938 an order was issued that gave the Army Air Corps responsibility for airborne anti-sub patrol within a distance of one hundred miles off the coast of the United States. The Navy patrolled beyond that.

Dad flew these patrols as a member of the 12th Anti-Submarine Squadron based at Langley Field, Virginia. The squadron flew the Douglas B-18B Bolo. In the mid-thirties the Douglas Aircraft Company designed the very successful DC-3 airliner. They took that basic airframe and developed two versions for military use. The bomber version was the B-18 and the cargo version was the famous C-47.

The installation of Magnetic Anomaly Detection, or MAD gear, essentially made the bomber a "flying metal detector." When a sub was detected a bag of aluminum powder called "slick" was dropped by one of the crew. This marked the location of the sub. The bomber then made a 180-degree turn and began its attack. The silvery slick gave the bombardier an aiming point. The weapon of choice against submarines was the depth charge. Nicknamed "ash cans" for their cylindrical shape, depth charges could be set to explode at a preset depth. There were three U-boat kills by B-18 Bolos. In the longest pursuit of a submarine by aircraft, U-615 was finally sunk in the Caribbean Sea on August 7, 1943. One of the aircraft scoring hits on her was a B-18 from the 10th Bomb Squadron based in Puerto Rico. On October 2, U-512 was sunk off the coast of French Guiana by a B-18 from the 99th Bomb Squadron. On October 30, a Royal Canadian Air Force Bolo sank U-520 off the coast of Newfoundland.

Dad describes the sinking of a U-boat by the U.S.S. Spence. It was actually a U.S. Coast Guard cutter, the U.S.S. Spencer (WPG-36), which sank the German U-boat U-175 on April 17, 1943. The U.S.S. Spence (DD-512) was a U.S. Navy destroyer. In the month of April, the Spence was on convoy duty off the coast of Africa.

In the course of my research, I found that Dad was incorrect as to the identity of the co-pilot on the "Silver Knight of the Skies" patrol. Lt. Charles Lofdahl was a bombardier and not a pilot. In 2008 I spoke to Herschel Smith. His memory was sharp. He remembered that the co-pilot on that patrol was Lt. William Ogden. Lt. Ogden also joined the 492nd BG and became the pilot and leader of Crew 606.

Dad flew his patrols from March to June of 1943. By this time the U-boat menace, though not eradicated, had been sharply reduced. As Dad says, the Navy took over the ASW mission.

While serving in the 12th Anti-Sub Squadron, Dad met Lt. Peter Val Preda. For the next 16 months they flew together as pilot and flight engineer almost exclusively. On May 17, they along with five others flew their B-18 from Langley Field, Virginia, to Pete's hometown of Rutland, Vermont. They "buzzed" the town a number of times before landing at the newly opened MacArthur Field. This caused quite a stir and was the subject of a front page article in the Rutland Herald.

The 12th Anti-Sub Squadron had flown their last patrol in their obsolete B-18s. All told, Dad accumulated 130 hours in the Bolo.

In the month of July and early August the squadron was equipped with B-25 Mitchell bombers, the same type used in the famous Doolittle raid. All flights were listed as training flights and no patrols were flown. I was confused by this and asked Herschel Smith. He replied that the B-25s just showed up one day and they began flying them. When I asked him his opinion of the B-25 he did not hesitate to say that, "North American [Aviation] never made a bad airplane. The B-25 was the best airplane I ever flew." A month later the B-25s were gone. In August Dad made his first flight in the airplane that would define his time in the service, the B-24 Liberator. Over the next 10 months he would accumulate 420 flight hours in the Lib.

In late September of 1943 the 12th Anti-Sub Squadron was transferred to Blythe, California, after nine months at Langley Field, Virginia. Dad made the trip by rail. He bought a "Serviceman's Map of the United States" for 10 cents and traced the route they took. The circuitous course covered 11 states. Dad jokes about an anti-sub unit being sent to the desert. At the time it must have seemed foolish. But when they got there the 12th Anti-Sub Squadron was disbanded. On October 1, it became the 859th Bomb Squadron, the nucleus of the 492nd Bomb Group.

Dad complains of their "easy days" coming to an end when the Maintenance Officer of the newly formed 859th Bomb Squadron volunteered them to work on the aircraft of another group. His recollection (after 57 years) of the "30th or 36th Bomb Group" was close, but it was actually the 34th Bomb Group. This group had been based at Blythe, California, as a training group. It was designated an operational bombardment group during this period. The 34th relocated to England and began combat operations within days of the 492nd. Dad doesn't describe what "2nd Air Force rules were stretched or broken to accomplish this." But having been in military aviation, I would surmise that some of the airplanes became what are called "hangar queens." These are aircraft that that have had so many components removed, or "cannibalized," to keep their sister ships in the air that they are no longer airworthy.

I hesitated to include Dad's criticism of General Longfellow. Whether or not it is warranted I don't know. But that was his perception of the situation. The General may well have been justified in his decision but the reasons were not evident to the men who had to obey them.

It was during this time that my parents met. Their story was a familiar one for the day. Four months after they were married, Dad left for England. Eighteen months would pass before they would be together again.

• • •

The 12th Anti-Sub Squadron flew the Douglas B-18 Bolo in the hunt for German U-Boats. (Ramsay Library, New England Air Museum)

CHAPTER 4
MEETING MY WIFE

I returned to Atlantic City after a weekend pass in New York City with Clarke Glazier. Upon our arrival we were met by Clarke's girlfriend Helen Klimek. A nice looking girl was waiting with Helen at the train station. Her name was Ethel Dvorsky. We still had time before we had to check in at the armory so the four of us went to a restaurant on Atlantic Avenue. So, being a lonely soldier, I made a pass and managed to make a date to see her at a later time. Helen was the secretary to Wynant Farr, the commander of the Civil Air Patrol. We shared Atlantic City's Bader Field with the CAP. Whenever I had an opportunity, I would check with Helen about Ethel. I found out that she came from Dorothy, New Jersey, was Czechoslovakian, and graduated from Egg Harbor High School. Helen was the valedictorian and Ethel was salutatorian. Her parents owned a chicken farm on 13th Avenue. The farm had 1,200 chickens.

One day Helen told me that Ethel was coming to town and wanted to see me. So Clarke and I went to Helen's apartment in Atlantic City. The four of us went out to a local eatery. I believe it was the Knights of Columbus, a meeting place for my outfit while off duty. There we enjoyed decent food at a good price, music, and dancing. We took the girls back to Helen's apartment and were invited up for coffee. I thought something good could come of this but coffee and conversation only followed. We had to report back to the armory. So as we were ready to leave Ethel came close to me and I seized the moment and kissed her not once but three times. She was a terrific kisser and I was hooked. We made plans for another date. She came to Atlantic City once a week for classes in auto mechanics. She was also an aircraft spotter in Dorothy. If the enemy got that far inland we were in real trouble.

Well, she was always on my mind, while Clarke was getting less interested in Helen. So Ethel and I would go out alone. On one pass she insisted I meet her parents. This was getting serious. I had a weekend pass in my pocket and she picked me up at the armory in her 1937 Ford sedan. We were off to Dorothy. While driving down Tuckahoe Road and having a conversation, she suddenly pulled the car over to the side of the road. Without saying a word she went to the trunk of the car. She pulled out a large can of oil and poured it into a quart container. She opened the hood and added the oil to the engine. She put everything away and wiped her hands on an old towel. Then restarting the car she picked up the conversation where she left off. While this is going on I'm sitting there with my mouth wide open and wondering what the hell is going on. I interrupted her and asked her how she knew her car needed oil immediately. I thought she was gifted with ESP like all Bohemians. Simple she said, her car uses a quart every fifty miles and we had just reached that milestone. She wasn't taking any chances of damaging the engine so she faithfully added oil at those intervals.

She needed the car to go to work in Vineland. She was the book-keeper, secretary, and baby sitter for a large poultry business. I believe they took advantage of her, paying her very little money for her services. Ethel told me at a later date that the owners of the company wished I had never met her. They were losing their coolie labor. I can't remember when but the Ford died sometime before we were married. If we needed a car after that Martin Masek, the Dvorsky's next door neighbor, would loan us his coupe. Martin and his wife Agnes were wonderful people to the Dvorsky and Centore families. We continued to date but in January 1943 our outfit was transferred to Langley Field, Virginia. So our visits stopped and letter writing became our form of communication.

By mid 1943 I became a flight engineer. By doing so I was required to go to gunnery school at Tyndall Field, Florida. After graduation we were given our travel orders to return to our bases. I figured I could sneak in a trip to New Jersey to visit Ethel and return to Langley Field with no-body the wiser. I got away with it. I don't remember the fine details but I continued beyond Virginia to Philadelphia. With my youthful looks and sergeant stripes I walked boldly through the terminal past countless military police and shore patrol. No one challenged me but just being there I was AWOL. I took the train to Dorothy and Ethel picked me up at the whistle stop station. I stayed two days and left for Langley Field with no questions asked or explanations necessary.

Returning to base I was thinking very much about Ethel. She made me feel comfortable. She was quiet and unassuming and we just hit it off. After about a week I realized this was the woman for me.

We had been hearing rumors that our days as an anti-sub squadron were numbered. The tactics were changing and the Navy was taking it over. Toward the end of August I was given a seven-day furlough. Ethel had moved to New York City and was living with my parents. She went to work for Western Electric in lower Manhattan. During those seven days I bought an engagement ring. When we took our blood tests Ethel passed out. Events were rushing by so fast that it might have been nerves or whatever. As she lay on the floor the nurses and I were making her comfortable. As she came to the first thing she did was pull her skirt down. It had been above her knee, what modesty.

Getting a priest to marry us became the bigger problem. The local pastor wouldn't do it because she had never been baptized. When I was asked why I wanted to marry her I said because I love her and want her for my wife. That wasn't the answer. So we tried two other churches outside my parish. We got the same answer from the first but the other priest gave us the clue we needed. He said to go to St. Patrick's Cathedral and see the military chaplain. We did so. After a few minutes with this priest he gave us the answer. I was to tell my parish priest that I was going to convert Ethel to the Catholic religion. We also had to sign a dispensation that any children would be raised as Catholics. We returned to the local priest and on September 5, 1943 we were married. The ceremony was done in the rectory and not in the church proper. Among the guests were my Aunt Tess and Uncle Jim and their son Carl, my friend Jimmy Madonna and his wife Louise. Tess was the maid of honor and Jimmy was my best man. Mom and Pop Centore rounded out my side. Ethel's whole family was there. Mom and Pop Dvorsky were joined by there three sons, Fred and his wife Julia, Lou and his wife Mary, and Joe who was a bachelor at that time. After the service we went to what else but an Italian restaurant. My brother-in-law Joe was a professional photographer and after the meal we went to his studio for pictures. We spent our wedding night at the Hotel Pennsylvania which was located across the street from Penn Station. The following day we left for Connecticut. We spent the night at the home of friends I had met when I worked at the Torrington Company before joining the Army. The following morning they knocked on the door and slipped a telegram under it. I had left my itinerary with the squadron so they could contact me if necessary. The telegram said that I was to return to base immediately. We returned to New York where I said goodbye to my wife boarded a train for Langley Field.

When I got there the outfit was in turmoil. We were packing everything up in preparation to ship out. We were all set to go but as usual something came up and it was a case of hurry up and wait. They had us move to very nice brick barracks where we sat around doing *nothing. I even played golf on the nine-hole course. For the next two weeks we played cards went to the movies and wrote letters. We were finally ordered to move out. If I knew we were going to hang around for this length of time I would have stayed with my new wife. Our destination was unknown when we boarded the troop train at Langley. Once underway we found out that we were going west to Blythe, California. We arrived there in October, 1943.*

After a couple of weeks at Blythe, orders came down for 60 ground and flight crews to be sent to Orlando, Florida, for ACT (Advanced Combat Training). We traveled by train in Pullman cars. Upon our arrival in Orlando we were assigned to barracks and informed our class would not start for another three weeks. Some of the fellows contacted their wives and asked them to come to Florida for a couple of weeks. I thought this was a great idea and contacted Ethel. We had been married the month before in New York. She got the time off work and came down. We stayed in a lovely home somewhere in Orlando until she had to return. We were able to spend a week together.

COMMENTARY

People on the home front were encouraged to do their part for the war effort. Many worked in the defense industry. Mom was an aircraft spotter. Spotters were trained in aircraft identification. When an airplane flew over they would consult their book of aircraft silhouettes. If they saw a German or Japanese airplane they would alert the authorities. Fighters would then be deployed to intercept them. Of course, no such call was ever made. But no doubt there were numerous false alarms.

In order to keep her Ford sedan going, Mom took a course in basic auto repair. With so many mechanics drafted into the service, car owners had to do a great deal of their own maintenance.

During World War II the Civil Air Patrol worked with the Army in patrolling for German submarines off the coast of the United States. In July, 1942 Dad was transferred to Atlantic City, New Jersey. The CAP commander on the base was Wynant Farr. On July 11, 1942 Farr and another pilot were patrolling 25 miles offshore. Farr spotted a U-boat at periscope depth. From an altitude of 100 feet, they approached their quarry from the rear. When the target was in the bombsight's crosshairs the pilot released the first depth charge. They circled around and made a second attack. An oil slick and floating debris on the surface was evidence of a victory.

My grandparents were hard-working immigrants from what was then the Austro-Hungarian Empire. In 1919 they lost an infant child in the world-wide influenza epidemic. My mother was the youngest of their four surviving children and the only girl. She was born in 1924. At that time the family was living in New York City where my grandfather supported the family with a vegetable pushcart. In the early days of the depression he had saved up enough for a down payment and bought a chicken farm in Dorothy, New Jersey. Once their kids moved out of the house, the two of them ran the farm by themselves. None of my three uncles had any interest in taking over the farm and the operation ceased in 1954.

· · ·

Mary, Ignatz, and Ethel Dvorsky in 1942. (Author)

CHAPTER 5
THE B-24 LIBERATOR

In August, 1943 the 12th Anti-Sub Squadron traded their B-18 Bolos for four-engine Consolidated B-24 Liberators. This was the machine Crew 601 would take into battle. The B-24 never achieved the notoriety of Boeing's B-17 Flying Fortress, but it flew faster and carried a larger bomb load. I have spoken to many veterans of U. S. Army Air Force. Generally speaking, B-24 vets acknowledge that the B-17 was a fine airplane but I never heard one say they he would have preferred to have flown in the Fortress. Veterans of the B-17, on the other hand, have nothing good to say about the B-24. When I told one B-17 ball turret gunner that my Dad had flown in the B-24, he said he felt sorry for him. Another dismissed the Liberators out of hand as "the boxes our airplanes came in."

Liberators were produced in higher numbers than any other American combat aircraft. Allen Blue, an authority on the B-24, pegs the number at 19,256. To put that into perspective, if all those airplanes were parked wingtip to wingtip, they would form a ribbon of aluminum over 400 miles long! The Ford Motor Company was licensed by Consolidated to produce the Liberator. Ford built a huge plant in Willow Run, Michigan dedicated to the bomber. In an incredible display of manufacturing ability, Ford rolled a Liberator out the door at a rate of one an hour, 24 hours a day, seven days a week. To build such a complex machine at that rate is truly a monument to American industry.

The B-24 was 67 feet long and had a wingspan of 110 feet. Empty, she weighed about 36,000 pounds. With bomb bays and fuel tanks loaded it topped out at 65,000 pounds. The B-24 was powered by four 1,200 horsepower Pratt & Whitney radial engines. At 20,000 feet and 215 miles per hour, the Liberator would consume over 200 gallons of fuel per hour. Climbing to altitude burned fuel at better than twice that rate. A typical mission over Germany burned over 2,000 gallons of high-octane gasoline.

There were four bomb bay doors on a B-24. Rather than opening outward, the doors slid up the sides of the aircraft, much like an old fashioned roll top desk. A typical bomb load was five to eight thousand pounds and was determined by the type of target to be attacked. Generally speaking, high explosive bombs broke up buildings and incendiary bombs set the rubble on fire.

The U. S. Eighth Air Force and British Bomber Command subjected Germany to bombardment around the clock. The British bombed by night, the darkness concealing them from the enemy's eyes. But the darkness also concealed relatively small targets such as industrial facilities, airfields, or railroad yards. To make up for this, the British conducted area bombing. Whole cities, rather than targets within them, were attacked.

By contrast, the American objective was the destruction of Germany's ability to wage war. Daylight precision bombing, it was argued, could and would destroy Germany's heavy industry, fuel production, and transportation system. The light of day allowed American bombardiers to pick out individual targets. But if the Americans could see their targets German fighter pilots and antiaircraft crews could also see the Americans. But no matter how many fighters came up to attack or no matter how heavy the antiaircraft fire, no American bomber mission was turned back due to the severity of enemy action.

The B-24 and B-17 were conceived in the late nineteen thirties. They were designed on the principle that a formation of bombers could defend itself from attack by enemy fighters. To accomplish this, bombers were armed with large caliber machine guns capable of firing in every direction. Given that bombers fly in large formations, a fighter attacking from any quarter would be in the sights of several gunners. This concept was borne of necessity. At that point in time fighters with sufficient range to escort bombers to distant targets were only on the drawing board.

In actual practice, the best way to defend bombers was to escort them to and from the target with a gaggle of long-range fighters. Bombing missions that suffered the greatest losses were most often due to a lapse in fighter cover when the bombers had to fend for themselves.

• • •

Each year the Collings Foundation brings their B-24 Liberator and B-17 Flying Fortress to over one hundred destinations. A visit to these historic aircraft is highly recommended. You'll have an opportunity to enter, and if you'd like, take a flight in these beautifully restored machines. (Jim Harley, Collings Foundation)

CHAPTER 6
CREW 601

The 492nd Bomb Group (BG) was comprised of four Bomb Squadrons: the 856th, 857th, 858th, and 859th. Each squadron had approximately 18 aircraft, though this number was fluid due to losses and replacements. The group arrived in England in April of 1944 with 70 aircraft and crews. Another 49 crews were assigned to the group to replace losses to German fighters and anti-aircraft fire. Crew 601, of the 856th Bomb Squadron, was formed at Alamogordo, New Mexico in January, 1944. The original crew was comprised of four officers and six enlisted men. From the time of its formation to the final mission 1st Lt. (later Captain) Peter Val Preda was its pilot. The other three officers were transferred to other crews when they got to England. The original copilot, Lt. Elvern Seitzinger, flew three missions with Crew 601 before getting his own crew. We are not sure who flew as copilot on the next four missions. On the crew's last mission Lt. Carey Walton was the co-pilot. The original bombardier, Lt. Luke Rybarczyk, was transferred to Crew 608. The original navigator, Lt. Norman Burns, was transferred to Crew 606. The bombardier and navigator shared tight quarters in the nose of the aircraft. To get to their station, they would enter through the bomb bay and crawl under the cockpit and around the retractable nose wheel. Often one of these two officers flew in the nose turret. Some crews preferred to have a trained gunner in the turret.

All six enlisted men originally assigned to the crew remained with Val Preda. The R/O (radio operator) was Technical Sergeant Walter Kean. He was a 39 year-old Pennsylvanian and the oldest man on the crew. Walt had enlisted in the pre-war Army and was in the cavalry Signal Corps before transferring to the Air Corps.

Technical Sergeant Nello Centore, 25, of New York City, was the flight engineer. He was trained in all aircraft systems and had responsibilities in several areas. He conferred with the maintenance crew chief to insure the aircraft was ready for flight. In-flight duties included fuel management, the transferring of fuel between the various tanks. As the engines could not draw fuel directly from the outer tanks, the transfer of fuel was rather critical. If an engineer did not do his job the engines stopped running! He was also an aerial gunner and operated the upper turret. After landing, the engineer opened a fuselage hatch and sat atop the aircraft. With an unobstructed view, he could provide taxiing instructions to the pilot.

The radio operator's table and flight engineer position were located on the command deck right behind the cockpit. A 10-inch wide catwalk at the bottom of the bomb bay connected the forward and rear areas of the aircraft. The catwalk was not only a walkway. It was part of the structure of the airplane, much like the keel of a ship.

To defend itself, the Liberator had ten .50 caliber Browning machine guns. Eight of them were installed in four motorized turrets. These were located in the nose, tail, upper fuselage, and a spherical ball turret on the bottom of the craft. The turrets were rotated, and their guns raised and lowered, by means of either hydraulic or electric motors. The gunner sat in the turret and rotated with it. Turret gun fire was automatically interrupted when the guns were pointing at the wing or tail of the aircraft. The ball turret gunner, the tail turret gunner, and the two waist gunners occupied the rear area of the airplane.

Staff Sergeant Douglas Pierce of Wilmer, Alabama, was the ball turret gunner. The ball turret was only 46 inches in diameter. With his bulky flying clothes, Pierce, who could not have suffered from claustrophobia, had to share this confined space with two machine guns, hydraulic motors, ammo chutes. Unlike the B-17's non-retracting turret, the ball turret on the B-24 retracted into the fuselage when not in use. This feature reduced drag and increased speed and range.

The tail gunner was Staff Sergeant Arthur St. Pierre of Manchester, New Hampshire. As you would expect, he defended against attacks from the rear. The nose and tail turrets were identical in the version of the Liberator Crew 601 flew.

Along with the ball and tail turret gunners, two waist gunners occupied the rear portion of the aircraft. Each waist gunner fired a single machine gun from an opening on the side of the rear fuselage. Chicago native Staff Sergeant Miles Toepper and Staff Sergeant Jack Reed of Springdale, Arkansas, manned the left and right waist guns, respectively. Unlike the motorized turrets, waist guns were moved manually. When the two waist gunners were firing, the sound has been described as two men with jackhammers working in a phone booth. Unlike the powered turrets, the waist guns had no interrupters. While tracking and firing at a fast moving enemy fighter, waist gunners had to be careful not to shoot parts of their own airplane.

The official crew photograph was taken in Alamogordo, New Mexico. Only nine members of the ten-man crew are in the picture. This was due to the fact that the B-24 was equipped with two five-man life rafts. This restricted the number of crewmen for the trans-oceanic flight to England to no more than ten. Ball turret gunner Miles Toepper was "bumped" off the flight in favor of Lt. Charles Lofdahl, one of the squadron's bombardiers. Sgt. Toepper sailed to England on the ocean liner Queen Elizabeth and had already departed for the ship when the photograph was taken.

• • •

This photograph of Crew 601 was taken at Alamogordo, New Mexico. Standing (L-R) are Pilot Peter Val Preda, Co-Pilot Elvern Seitzinger, Navigator Norman Burns, and Bombardier Luke Rybarczyk. Kneeling (L-R) are Engineer Nello Centore, Radio Operator Walter Kean, Tail Gunner Arthur St. Pierre, Ball Turret Gunner Douglas Pierce, and Waist Gunner Jack Reed. (USAF)

CHAPTER 7
THE FORMATION OF THE 492ND BOMB GROUP

On November 1, 1943 we started Advanced Combat Training (ACT). The training consisted of classes, lectures, and tours. We covered formation flying, air-to-air and air-to-ground gunnery. All missions were as close to wartime conditions as possible.

The training culminated with a "combat" mission to Kingston, Jamaica. We remained overnight under jungle conditions. We refueled the aircraft with hand pumps from 55-gallon drums. We also completed any required service and maintenance. Sleeping on the ground in the jungle was not my cup of tea, so I stretched out my lamb's wool-lined flight suit in the aft compartment of the aircraft and slept on it. The next morning I woke up with a sore throat that was a couple of octaves higher than a whisper. We went through the briefings for our simulated combat mission, which was to drop bombs on a shipwreck lying on a sandbar in an atoll. We flew at 20,000 feet and were told to watch for fighter interception. Well into the flight we were attacked by a squadron of P-47 Thunderbolts. We tracked them with our guns and proceeded to our target. After dropping 100-pound practice bombs on the ship we flew back to Orlando. Now I've got a problem. I can't swallow enough to pop my eardrums. I asked the pilot (and 492nd BG Commander), Lt. Col. Louis Adams, if he could decrease altitude in a series of steps so I could keep my ears popped. He did and when we landed in Orlando the flight surgeon medicated me for badly inflamed ears and throat. By the time we left Orlando my medical problems were corrected.

Upon completing ACT in December, I was transferred to Alamogordo, New Mexico. I was given a seventeen-day delay en route to get there. I took advantage of this and went from Florida to New Mexico by way of New York City to spend time with Ethel and the rest of my family. My oldest son Rick was conceived during this leave. As fate would have it, I was notified of his birth nine months later as a POW in Germany. I left New York by train the day after Christmas.

On the way to Alamogordo there was a layover in Chicago, Illinois. In Chicago I called my Aunt Lena and Uncle Joe. I was traveling with my *friend Leonard Ray and asked him to join us. The four of us had dinner at a restaurant and went to a movie. Leonard and I left the next morning.*

Arriving at Alamogordo we found out that we were the cadre for a new bomb group. We were assigned temporary living quarters. We also found out that we were not being joined by our ground crew. They were being sent to Salinas, Kansas, for Boeing B-29 training. Working out of a temporary office, I became a clerk doing one-finger typing of memos as dictated by Lt. Col. Adams. Lt. Col. Eugene Snavely was appointed permanent Commander of the 492nd BG in January, 1944. So I became his office boy and chaser until we formed up as a group. Adams became his Deputy Commander.

When we were assigned to Alamogordo we had no specific aircraft assigned to us. We needed to get some flight time to qualify for flight pay. Val Preda and Frank Haag went to the Maintenance Office to inquire if any aircraft needed check flights. There was one ready. John Crowley and I went along with them. I completed the preflight inspection on the aircraft with John's assistance. After checking out the engines we taxied to the runway. This aircraft was to be checked for flight control problems. After takeoff everything was working fine. Pete and Frank decided to fly by auto-pilot. While they talked about landing the airplane with the auto-pilot John and I were enjoying the scenery. After a couple of hours they decided to shoot some landings. We were on final approach. John asked if he could sit in the engineer's seat. I said OK and sat at the left cabin blister window watching the ground getting closer. Suddenly, from a normal glide, the aircraft went into a left bank and I had a vertical view of the ground. Pete and Frank yelled out for right aileron, rudder, and elevator. Like the incident with the B-18 the aircraft seemed to just hang in the air. The ground was now very close. At the last possible moment the aircraft responded to the controls, we rolled right and at same time were over the runway. The aircraft was now under control and we made a perfect landing. As we taxied to the end of the runway Pete said to Frank, "That was pretty interesting. Should we try it again?" John sat down in the radio operator's seat. I moved up between the two pilots and said that when we reached the control tower they should slow up. Pete asked why and I said, "Because that's where I'm getting off!" Something is still not right with the flight controls. At landing speed the controls lost their effectiveness. I felt that more investigation of the problem was needed. Pete agreed and taxied to the depot and wrote up a maintenance report. We called it a day.

There were two B-24 groups going through phase training at the time. When one left we took over their area. Now we were coming together as a full bomb group. Crews started arriving from Davis-Monthan Field in Arizona and Casper, Wyoming. Of the entire group, 32 crews failed Operational Readiness Inspection and were exchanged with crews from Biggs Field, Texas.

On March 17th we flew a practice mission for the infamous General Newton Longfellow. The General returned a week later for a full-dress Preparation for Overseas Movement (POM). We passed the first time and overseas movement began immediately. On April 4th we departed Alamogordo, New Mexico, and flew to Herington, Kansas. We stayed there a few days while combat equipment modifications were made to the aircraft.

COMMENTARY

The group was one of the few to pass the POM inspection the first time and ahead of schedule. Prior to leaving the States the group flew their brand new Liberators to Herington, Kansas, for additional armor plating and other modifications deemed necessary for combat in the skies over Europe. Now the pace was really picking up. The crew arrived at Herington on April 3 and left for West Palm Beach, Florida on April 8. They only had two days to make final preparations for the long over-water flights that would bring them to the United Kingdom.

Dad's flight records have no entries for November of 1943. I asked Herschel Smith about this and he did not believe they did any flying in that month. Many of the men went on their last leave before departing for the ETO, the European Theater of Operations. Many of the families would never see their husbands, sons, and brothers again. As Dad states he was able to get one more leave at Christmas, which as he also states was very fortunate for me. This would be the last time Mom and Dad would see each other until June of 1945. By the end of the month they had begun ACT, Advanced Combat Training.

In the test hop incident, Dad mentions Lt. Frank Haag and S/Sgt John Crowley. They were members of Crew 611 of the 856th Bomb Squadron. Frank was the pilot and crew leader and John was the tail gunner. There were two Haag brothers in the 492nd, Frank and George, and they were identical twins. In what was most likely an unusual assignment, both were pilots in the same group. George commanded Crew 706 of the 857th Bomb Squadron. After 22 round trips, luck ran out for Crew 611 on the disastrous July 7 mission to Bernberg, Germany. Overall, the 492nd lost 12 aircraft with 67 killed and 52 were taken prisoner. George also flew this mission and watched his brother's plane get hit and go down. Four men on the crew were killed and six became prisoners of war including Frank Haag and John Crowley.

George Haag's crew was fortunate. They survived 25 missions including the four worst: Brunswick, both missions to Politz, and Bernberg where his brother Frank was shot down. George's crew was transferred to the 44th BG after the 492nd was disbanded.

Dad refers to General Newton Longfellow as "infamous." This was his second reference to the General. Longfellow was in charge of training bases in the southwest. Two of them were Blythe, California, and Alamogordo, New Mexico. Dad felt that some of the policies promulgated by the General caused the loss of aircraft and men. This might or might not be true but it was his, and probably others', perception.

The railroads had a monumental task in moving troops and war material around the country. In September the 12th Anti-Sub Squadron was transferred to the west coast where it became the nucleus of the 492nd Bomb Group. Dad took the train from Langley Field, Virginia, to Blythe, California. One month later in October he was on his way east to Orlando, Florida, for Advanced Combat Training. In December he was on the rails again, this time from Orlando, Florida, to Alamogordo, New Mexico. During the last trip he and Leonard Ray enjoyed the stopover at Aunt Lena's home in Chicago. Dad and Leonard had been flight engineers in the 12th Anti-Sub Squadron. When the 492nd formed up, Leonard Ray became the flight engineer for Lt. David McMurray. They were originally part of the 858th Bomb Squadron as Crew 801. They became the hard-luck crew in the hard-luck outfit. Their bad luck began on their fifth mission. On May 29 the ball turret gunner, Sgt. Pat Tracey, was killed on the Group's first mission to Politz. Nine days after D-Day, on June 15, the crew flew its 12th mission. Their B-24 was shot down and the crew bailed out near the front lines in France. All the men made it to the allied positions and were returned to England. After the decimation of the 856th Squadron June 20 the McMurray crew was reassigned as Crew 602. They flew three missions as such but their bad luck returned on the tragic Bernberg mission on July 7. They were shot down and the entire crew was declared killed in action. Their fate was unknown until Enrico Schwartz, a German civilian, discovered the remains in 2001. After thorough investigation and DNA analysis the remains were identified. Leonard Ray was buried in his home state of Maryland on October 5, 2007. Dad passed away six days later.

•   •   •

CHAPTER 8
THE FLIGHT TO ENGLAND

The next stop was Morrison Field in West Palm Beach, Florida. We departed the United States on Easter Sunday morning, April 9, 1944. Our pilot, Pete Val Preda, had done a hitch in the Navy. During his hitch he had crossed the equator and went through the traditional ceremony to become a "shellback." When we crossed the equator over South America Pete performed a modified ritual using our canteen water supply that made us official shellbacks. We landed in Trinidad during their monsoon season. The rain was not drops but a wall of water. We were billeted in an open air cabin and slept under mosquito netting. The food was nothing to write home about. The next stop was Belem, Brazil. There was monsoon rain there too.

This was becoming a very interesting trip. From Belem we flew to Natal, Brazil. The number three engine needed some fine tuning. While I worked on the aircraft the rest of the crew spent time at the beach. We laid over for a couple of days. I talked to the locals as best I could. They spoke Portuguese and I spoke a limited Italian. We then left for Dakar, Senegal, in western Africa. The navigators were cautioned to fly by celestial navigation rather than relying on radio beam signals. German U-Boats would lie in wait somewhere in the Atlantic Ocean and transmit erroneous signals. A lazy navigator would home in on them until the fuel ran out and the aircraft would still be over the open ocean. We had a very good navigator in Lt. Norman Burns. We flew such a direct course that when we made landfall, Pete made a straight in approach, right to the runway. As the main gear made contact with the runway I thought the aircraft was disintegrating. There was no problem. It was simply my first experience with a runway made of PSP (pierced steel planking).

I was very interested in cruise control, the management of engine power settings to maximize range. We followed the factory recommended settings religiously. After servicing the aircraft in Dakar I found we had used less than 2,000 gallons of fuel. That evening at the PX I spoke to other flight engineers and found out that many had used 200 to 400 gallons more than we did. When I told Pete this he was impressed with the results. Our aircraft was very efficient. But even with the conscientious application of cruise control it averaged less than one mile per gallon.

The pass through the Atlas Mountains was covered in clouds. So we stayed in Dakar for two days until the weather cleared. We went to the beach where locals were fishing or cooking their food. The Senegalese are very dark-skinned—more black than brown. By the second day the weather cleared over the mountains. With the improved weather we were able to leave Senegal for Marrakech, Morocco. As we flew over the field prior to landing we saw our first B-29s. There were many of them. They were parked away from the area we were to be located at. My friend Arthur St. Pierre took many pictures of them.

We landed and secured the aircraft. After servicing we were taken to our billets. They were tents located in an olive grove. On the way we passed an Italian POW camp. They were guarded by the meanest looking Senegalese soldiers. They had fixed bayonets that looked like they were three feet long. We were held up again by bad weather. This time it was over England and the English Channel. So I used my time talking in my limited Italian to the POWs. Everyone told me they had cousins in Brooklyn. They had been given pieces of aluminum and wood. With their artistic ability they were able to make some rather nice things. An officer was trying to buy a model of a P-38 mounted on a pedestal. It was very well done. He asked me to interpret for him. The officer was offering money but the POW wanted clothes, a shirt or pair of pants he could wear because his clothes were threadbare. I told the officer, "Look, just go to the PX and buy some clothing. It would be cheaper. What can he do with money?" The officer was adamant so I told him to forget the P-38 and walked away. He was ticked off because I wouldn't do any more for him.

I returned to my aircraft only to find that I had my own problems there. Our fuel tanks were filled to the brim and the heat of sun caused the expanding fuel to leak out of the vent lines. I wasn't the only one with this problem. The air was saturated with fuel fumes. I yelled to crew members of other aircraft, "Don't smoke, and pass the word to everyone." To relieve the pressure on the fuel cells, I popped our fuel caps. Fuel just gushed over the wing and onto the desert floor. Now the fumes were their greatest. One spark, or one match, and a whole air force would be lost. Arthur St. Pierre, Jack Reed, and Douglas Pierce came out to our aircraft. They checked out their equipment. Reed was my assistant engineer. He had obtained some cheese cloth-like material, which he put over the filler necks to keep dirt out of the tanks. The fuel caps were laid on top to hold the cloth in place. Later in the day, the danger passed and the air cleared.

The fuel drains were checked to see if sand had gotten into the tanks while the caps were off. We were lucky. Everything was fine. We secured the aircraft but did not top off the tanks in case we were stuck there for another day. We were notified by Pete that we would be leaving the next morning. I informed him of the fuel situation, suggesting we wait until tomorrow to top off the tanks. Pete agreed to delay serving the aircraft as plans could change.

That afternoon the B-29s were gone. India was their destination. While they were there Pete met a B-29 pilot he had gone to flight school with. Pete was given the grand tour of the new bomber. He was very impressed with what he saw. I got the impression he would have liked reassignment to the B-29.

Our spare time was spent in our tents but we did get into the city of Marrakech. We took a horse and carriage ride down the main drag and through the bazaar section. I spent more time talking to the Italian POWs. My Italian language skills were improving because of this. It's too bad I wasn't sent to a 15th Air Force outfit in Italy.

The next morning we left Marrakech for Valley, Wales. The navigator was again cautioned to use standard navigation procedures rather than follow radio beams. If you look at a map you will notice that Valley, Wales, and the Brest peninsula of France have an almost identical coastline. Some crews mistook France for Wales and landed on a German airfield only to become POWs. Then the Germans would have a fully intact B-24 or B-17.

Our flight to Wales was uneventful. The officers were sent to the officer's billet. Our Radio Operator Walter Kean and I were sent to a Quonset hut occupied by three RAF airmen. One was an Aussie, one was an ANZAC (New Zealander), and one was an Englishman. The rest of the hut was empty. Reed, Pierce, and St. Pierre were billeted elsewhere and we didn't see them until we departed for our permanent airbase. While Walt and I were getting our bunks made the RAF airmen invited us to join them at the Sergeant's mess. Once there they insisted we were not to pay for anything. Everything was on them so Walt and I began drinking our first English beer. The RAF boys ran out of money. I said no problem and gave the barmaid an American $5 bill. I said for her to keep sending the beer to our table. She could work out the exchange rate and when that ran out I'd give her more. When the Mess closed, five very drunk airmen staggered out leaning on each other.

There was a blackout to prevent German night bomber attacks. As such, we could never have found our hut had it not been for our RAF friends. They poured us into our bunks and flopped into theirs. When we awoke the RAF boys were gone. We never saw them again and I always wondered how they made out. It was a memorable night. Three RAF men showed us a great kindness and camaraderie that I remember to this day. I hope God was good to them.

We left Wales that morning and two hours later we arrived at our new base, North Pickenham, England. Our combat life was about to begin.

COMMENTARY

Dad's memory was pretty good here. The actual date they left the States was Monday, April 10, 1944. The 492nd took the southern route to reach the United Kingdom. The journey was broken into seven legs. After 12 days the crew arrived at their base in North Pickenham, England on April 22. The trip covered over 10,000 miles and took 59 flying hours.

The departure point was Morrison Field in West Palm Beach, Florida. The first leg took 11 hours and brought them to the Caribbean island of Trinidad. They made two stops in Brazil. The first was at Belem. The second was at Natal, their last stop in the Western Hemisphere.

The route from Natal to Dakar, Senegal, is the shortest distance between the continents of South America and Africa. The 1,800-mile flight was the longest one the crew ever flew. They spent over 12 hours in the air.

The very able navigator of Crew 601, Lt. Norman Burns, was correct to do celestial navigation and not rely on homing in on a radio station. In his book 32 Co-pilots, Dick Bastien tells of meeting a friend in Marrakech, Morocco who had been piloting a C-47 across the South Atlantic. A B-24 could make the Natal to Dakar flight in one hop. But the shorter range of the C-47 necessitated a refueling stop at Ascension Island, a 35-square mile speck in the South Atlantic Ocean. The C-47 crew was homing in on what they thought was the island's radio beacon. The signal was actually emanating from a German submarine. The beacon went off the air and they droned on— lost. They ran out of fuel and had to ditch the plane in the sea. Luckily, the men were picked up by a passing ship.

The group displayed their competence again as all 73 aircraft touched down at their new home without losing any of them. That was a first for the Eighth Air Force. Now that the group was at their home base of North Pickenham it was time to start earning their keep.

• • •

Lt. Colonel Eugene Snavely (fourth from right) brings the 492nd Bomb Group to its new home in North Pickenham, England. (C. Halbert)

CHAPTER 9
NORTH PICKENHAM

Within a few days all the crews checked in. Now the orientation classes started. Among other subjects we were taught escape and evasion. Security was drilled into us. There was to be no idle chatter about where we went or were going. Loose lips lose aircraft and men.

Our crew chief was a young man from Kentucky or Tennessee. His assistant wasn't too sharp but he would follow his chief's orders and the aircraft was always ready for a combat or training flight. We flew practice missions to sharpen formation flying and other things necessary for a successful mission. On one such mission General Leon Johnson flew as our command pilot. Regardless of his high rank, he was very easy to talk to. Walt Kean was 39 at that time and the General remarked about his age. He offered Walt a transfer to the 44th Bomb Group Headquarters if Walt wanted it. But Walt said he had trained with us squirts and was going to stay with us. Walt had been a radioman in the prewar cavalry which was part of the Signal Corps. General Johnson abided by his decision. That decision was to cost Walt his right leg a few weeks later.

We flew diversionary flights to mislead the Germans. For example, we would fly toward the French coast then turn north or south and then fly dog-leg patterns on our return to base. When it was determined we were ready, we flew a full dress rehearsal for General Jimmy Doolittle. He was said to show great pleasure in our performance. We were given the go-ahead to begin combat operations.

COMMENTARY

It had only been six months since the group began forming back in October. Throughout their training the group had shown great potential. Now they were part of the Eighth Air Force and about to put that potential into practice.

The group started flying diversionary training flights in early May. Crew 601 flew on six such missions. Dad mentioned that General Leon Johnson (1904-1997) flew one of them with Crew 601. The General had won the Medal of Honor for his role as commander of the 44th Bomb Group in the famous low-level mission to Ploesti, Romania, on August 1, 1943. In May 1944 he was the commander of the Eighth Air Force's 14th Combat Wing, which was made up of the 44th, 392nd, and 492nd Bomb Groups. Dad's praise of Johnson was widespread. He was held in high esteem by all of his officers and men. James Mahoney, the commander of the 859th Squadron, describes Johnson as reminding one more of a college professor than an Air Force general. Mahoney never heard the general raise his voice or become excited, even when circumstances warranted it. In the course of my research I have never read one word of criticism of General Johnson.

In regard to the General's query to Walt Kean asking if he wanted to transfer to headquarters, the implication is that Kean was too old to fly combat. It is a bit surprising as Kean and Johnson were the same age. General Jimmy Doolittle, the commander of the Eighth Air Force and a winner of the Medal of Honor for leading the famous "Doolittle Raid" on Japan, was eight years older than Johnson.

On May 11th the group would receive its baptism of fire. Mission number one for the 492nd Bomb Group would be the railroad marshalling yards at Mulhouse, France. Crew 601 would lead the group on its first foray into combat.

• • •

CHAPTER 10
First Mission
May 11, 1944

Our first mission was the marshalling yards in Mulhouse, France. We were awakened at 11:30 P.M. We washed, shaved, and dressed in our heated flying suits. We ate a breakfast of real eggs. We assembled in the Operations Room for target briefing. After this each section went to their respective areas for additional briefings. Arthur St. Pierre, Jack Reed, Miles Toepper, Douglas Pierce, and I went out to the hardstand where our aircraft was parked. The crew chief and I did the preflight checks. We ran the engines and found all systems OK. After shutdown we called for the fuel truck and topped off all tanks including aux tanks. We carried 2,750 gallons in total. I entered the aircraft and checked my turret for operation and guns for ammunition.

By this time the officers along with our Radio Operator Walt Kean had finished their briefings and came out to the aircraft. The officers were Lt. Peter Val Preda (pilot), Lt. Elvern Seitzinger (co-pilot), Lt. Luke Rybarczyk (bombardier), and Lt. Norman Burns (navigator). Also flying with us as Mission Command Pilot was our Group Commander Lt. Col. Eugene Snavely. The formation was made up of three squadrons. We were the lead squadron. Quite a bit of fuel was burned in the climb to altitude and organizing the formation. Before we departed for the French coast I transferred fuel from the aux tanks to the mains. It was a timed procedure that took approximately 12 minutes per tank. We fell in behind the bomb group ahead of us. We crossed the Channel and flew into France. We started getting flak soon after that. I heard a whining sound as I turned the turret forward. Just ahead and above us a shell exploded, and the whining sound stopped. I always thought this shell was aimed directly at us. Lucky for us the German gunners were high and forward. Otherwise they would have hit us square in the bomb bay. We encountered no more flak or enemy fighters on our way to the target.

When we started on our bomb run the target was completely covered with smoke. The Germans used smoke generators to accomplish this. Snavely ordered the bombs held and ordered the group to circle the area, not once, but three times looking for an opening. When none appeared we flew back across France. Along the way he had the Bombardier drop the group's bombs on a small railroad track line. What a waste. Val Preda was very disgusted but couldn't say anything. After all, the Group CO was in command.

When we crossed the coastline Lt. Shalvoy (Crew 618) asked permission to break away because he was low on fuel. Permission was granted and they ran out of gas as they attempted to land at a B-17 base. In the ensuing crash the navigator (Lt. George Metzger) was killed. He was the first 492nd BG casualty. The pilot, engineer, and radio operator were injured and returned to the United States. The bombardier, co-pilot, and gunners were not injured and were reassigned to other crews.

We were not happy campers after our return to base. All of that was for nothing. We felt Snavely screwed up. Dropping bombs on a field and a one-track rail line was no way to win a war, or begin your operational life. We were not proud of this day. To add insult to injury, we did not get the shot of Scotch whiskey we were supposed to at the mission briefing. Our illustrious ground officers drank it. They said they were sweating us out and drank the scotch to settle their nerves—what a crock.

As a lead crew we stood down for a few days. (Note: In this case it was only two days.) About that time we bought bicycles so we could easily travel around the base and beyond. We even found a couple of places that sold us eggs for 60 cents a dozen.

COMMENTARY

For their first foray against the Third Reich, the 492nd Bomb Group dispatched 30 Liberators with Crew 601 in the lead. In his description of it Dad doesn't discuss the grand strategy of the allied bombing campaign. His concerns are personal: breakfast and the status of the aircraft. His recollection was very good although he was incorrect about which aircraft they flew. Pete Val Preda had signed for the brand new unpainted silver B-24J Liberator 44-40163 in Alamogordo, New Mexico. The crew trained in it and flew it across the Atlantic to England. They considered it "their airplane" even though this was not exclusive. If an aircraft was available and its primary crew was not scheduled to fly, another crew would be assigned to it. Crews 610, 613, and R-06 also flew combat missions in 44-40163. Crew 601 flew their first and sixth mission in an olive drab B-24J named "Little Lulu," number 42-110142. Little Lulu was the one of the last Liberators to sport a paint job. Deleting paint not only saved weight, the smooth surface of the natural metal reduced parasitic drag. The 492nd BG was the first group to have a majority of its aircraft in natural metal finish. In attempting to explain the heavy losses of this group, there has been speculation that German fighters specifically sought out the "silver airplanes" for attack. There could be some substance to this. However, the Eighth Air Force regularly sent up hundreds of bombers every day. It's hard to believe that the Luftwaffe would ignore scores of other aircraft in order to pounce on the silver Liberators of the 492nd, which never numbered more than 40 on any one mission.

When a bomb group went into combat, a Mission Command Pilot flew in the lead aircraft. The term pilot in this case is a bit of a misnomer. Mission Commander would be more correct. His seat was behind the pilot and co-pilot and he would direct the air battle. On this day Crew 601 led the group. The Mission Command Pilot was the Commanding Officer of the 492nd, Lt. Col. Eugene Snavely. In addition to Lt. Burns, a second navigator, Lt. John Smith, flew this mission as Group Lead Navigator. Smith had been a navigator with Pan American Airlines before the war and had an excellent reputation for accuracy. The 492nd flew in the "tail end Charlie" position behind the other two groups of the 14th Combat Wing, the 44th and the 392nd. When the bomb run began, Smith told Snavely that the railroad yards in the town they were about to strike were not in Mulhouse, France. Snavely had a tough decision to make: either bomb the same target as the veteran groups or trust Smith and find a secondary objective. Complicating the matter was the fact that Mulhouse is less than 20 miles from Switzerland. The attacking force had been specifically warned to avoid the neutral nation. Snavely had the group circle the area three times before opting for another target. Major James Mahoney described a very tense post-mission meeting with the 14th Combat Wing Commander, General Leon Johnson, but Smith stuck to his guns. During the meeting the General was called to the telephone. He was told that strike photographs proved Smith had it right! The other groups had indeed bombed Belfort, France, and not Mulhouse. Snavely was correct to have trusted Smith's judgment in that the target was not Mulhouse. But as it turned out the other groups didn't err too badly after all. Two weeks later the 492nd flew Mission 9. In an ironic twist, the target was the railroad yards at Belfort, France. There were no losses or casualties.

In the end, Val Preda was not alone in his frustration with the results of the mission. Colonel Snavely's indecisiveness, although justified by events, did not sit well with many of the crews. This seems harsh in light of Snavely's vindication. In researching the history of the 492nd BG one finds little praise for the Group Commander. This does seem unfair in that he oversaw the successful organization and training of the unit and brought it safely to England.

• • •

CHAPTER 11
Second Mission
May 13, 1944

This mission was to Tutow, Germany. It was a Focke-Wolfe aircraft assembly plant. Rising, eating, and dressing for the mission was pretty much the same as our first mission. After assembly over England we flew eastward. We crossed into Germany with an escort of P-38 Lightnings. As they flew cover above us, the flyboys started to do skywriting. They made the Eighth Air Force symbol in the sky above us with the contrails produced at high altitude. It's too bad no one ever had a snapshot of the event – great propaganda.

After the bomb drop we headed back toward the Baltic Sea. We were told we would pass over a newly built POW camp. If I'm not mistaken it was Stalag Luft IV, my future home. As we passed over there was only one compound. Two months later it was full and covered four compounds. More internees were coming in every day. On our return to base we did receive our shot of scotch at the debriefing.

Between missions we had G-2 intelligence briefings on escape and evasion and the latest German tactics. One tactic was to follow the bomber formation back to England. This didn't happen often, being forewarned, everyone kept alert until safely on the ground. Another tactic of German fighters was to hide in our contrails, pop up for a fast attack, and drop back down into to the contrails. One had to be alert at all times or you would be dead meat. Of course when we ran into a flak barrage there's not much you can do but hold your position and take your lumps.

We lost some of our people when they were forced to ditch or bail out in the English Channel. Air/Sea Rescue couldn't always get there in time. German E-Boats also roamed the Channel trying to pick up survivors.

Between missions we took off for the countryside. We stopped at the pubs and drank the English beer which is served at room temperature. I liked talking to the local residents. On one occasion I had an interesting conversation with some survivors of the Dunkirk evacuation. Much of our spare time was spent foraging for food. During the evening we were usually hungry and would fire up the pot-bellied stove. A local bakery truck made deliveries of cake and bread to the base. We would buy bread and make toast. We took butter from the mess hall and using our mess kit as a frying pan cooked the fresh eggs we had bought. Pierce caught a rabbit, skinned it, and cleaned it. He made a rabbit stew. I didn't eat any because I was told by my father that early spring rabbit could be wormy. But Pierce suffered no ill effects from his concoction.

Being a lead crew, we were not scheduled for many consecutive missions. Time was sometimes heavy on our hands. I used to hang out at the aircraft with the crew chief, looking over the plane and its maintenance records and generally killing time. Even with the amount of spare time I had I couldn't get anyone to paint a name on our aircraft. It was to be named "Pete's Pirates," along with a picture of a pirate. Our crew chief couldn't scrounge any paint. I guess it would have been better to have gotten it done in the States. No one seemed eager to participate even to only get the name painted. So our baby was never officially christened.

In May we had a three-day pass. We took a train to London and stayed at a Red Cross facility on Edgeware Road. We spent time at the Red Cross Canteen, visited Westminster Abbey, and saw the changing of the guard at Buckingham Palace. St. Pierre was my guardian angel during pub visits as he neither smoked nor drank.

After we returned to the base we found out from some guys that were just going on pass that we had been hit hard at Brunswick (492nd Mission 5 - 5/19/44) and that one of the dead was a crew member that joined the Air Corps the same time I as did. We were together at Fort Devens, Fort Dix, and the old 104th Observation Squadron. It was so sad because he was a very happy and funny Irishman named Pat Tracey. He was buried in the military cemetery in Cambridge. We had a truckload of his buddies in attendance at his funeral. It took an act of Congress and the intervention of some of our officers to convince Col. Snavely to allow us to go. We were very appreciative of our officers for their help in making this trip for one of our comrades.

COMMENTARY

Curtailing German aircraft production was a high priority for the Eighth Air Force. The destruction of the Luftwaffe would allow Allied Air Forces to roam free across the continent. The Focke-Wolfe operation at Tutow was a major producer of fighter planes. Their most formidable product was the FW-190. This high-performance aircraft could hold its own against the famous P-51 Mustang, considered by many to be the finest American fighter of the Second World War.

On this, the third mission for the 492nd, Lt. Col. Snavely flew as Mission Command Pilot with Crew 806. The group put up forty aircraft arranged in three sections. The lead section with Snavely was up front. Behind them were the low left and high right sections. The latter included Crew 601. When they got to the target area it was obscured by clouds. Snavely ordered the group to hold the bombs and circle around for another crack at it. The lead section complied but the other sections saw an opening and it was "bombs away." They followed the lead section as it circled around so as not to break up the formation. On the second pass, the lead section still didn't have a clear sight of the target. Snavely opted to abandon the original target and seek out targets of opportunity. As they flew over the west coast of Denmark, they unloaded on what Dick Bastien, co-pilot of Crew 714, called "fishing shacks." For whatever reason, one does not find the criticism of Snavely's penchant for circling the target that followed the Mulhouse mission.

From his perch in the upper turret, Dad would have been in the best position to see the P-38 pilots drawing the Eighth Air Force symbol with their contrails. It would indeed have made a good publicity photograph for the folks back home. Contrails form behind aircraft at high altitudes as water vapor condenses and freezes. These aerial "footprints" lead enemy fighters right to the bomber stream.

On the return to England the group did fly over a POW camp that would become Dad's home. But it was not Stalag Luft IV which was located much farther west of the mission's flight path. It was Stalag Luft I, located in Barth, Germany, a city on the coast of the Baltic Sea. Dad was originally sent to Stalag Luft IV, which was an enlisted men's camp. In January 1945 that camp had to be abandoned because of the advancing Russian Army. At that time he was moved to Stalag Luft I, an officers' camp.

The word "flak," which has become part of the American vernacular, is derived from flugabwehrkanone, the German term for anti-aircraft artillery. The 88 millimeter gun could fire a twenty pound shell over 30,000 feet in the air. This was more than adequate against Allied bomber fleets. If you were attacked by fighters you could shoot back or the escort fighters could engage them. But as Dad says, when flak came up you couldn't do anything but take your lumps. Bombers flew in formations not only for bombing accuracy but to maximize their defensive firepower with interlocking fields of fire. But unfortunately there was no defense against flak.

The idea of landing a B-24 in the water, or ditching, was a very dangerous proposition. The force of water at over 100 miles per hour is staggering. Boeing B-17 crews had a much higher survival rate, some say 10 times better, due to the fact that the B-17 wing is mounted low on the fuselage. When a B-17 struck the water the aircraft would skip along the surface, reducing the speed gradually. The wing on the B-24 was mounted high on the fuselage. This meant the fuselage would strike the water first. This, in turn, set off a violent train of events that seldom had a successful conclusion. The innovative bomb bay doors which slid up the side of the fuselage like a roll top desk were easily ripped off by the force of the water. The rush of water into the fuselage would break the back of the Liberator. In the abrupt deceleration, the heavy upper turret would break loose of its mountings and land on the pilot and co-pilot, oftentimes with fatal results. The only other choice would be to bail out and hope for rescue. Neither was a pleasant prospect.

Dad's friend Pat Tracey of Bayonne, New Jersey, was the ball turret gunner on Crew 801. He was KIA on the first Politz mission on May 29, not on the Brunswick mission 10 days earlier. In Reluctant Witness, Major James Mahoney shares Dad's fond memories of Pat Tracey. Mahoney describes the outcome of Tracey's last flight. As the aircraft approached the field the crew fired red flares as a signal that they had wounded aboard. This gave them priority to land as soon as possible. The ball turret in a B-24 retracts into the aft fuselage. But as this aircraft came in the turret was jammed in the "down" position, with S/Sgt. Tracey in it. This meant that pilot David McMurray had to land the aircraft in a level attitude to keep from dragging the turret on the tarmac. He did this well. But it was all for naught. A cannon shell had struck the turret and Tracey had died at his post. The reluctance by Col. Snavely to allow the enlisted men to go to Tracey's memorial service is unexplainable. But it is another negative reference to the Commanding Officer.

Dad mentions his disappointment that their aircraft was never officially named. A name gives an inanimate object an identity that a mere serial number cannot convey. There was more than enough time to get a name painted on the airplane. In fact, of the 70 original 492nd aircraft, only 11 had no name or nose art.

The crew considered naming the airplane after pilot Pete Val Preda with the alliterative moniker "Pete's Pirates." Author Robert Laird wrote that Pete told him he had planned to name his airplane after his first-born child. Unfortunately, on the day Diana Joan Val Preda was born on June 27, 1944, Liberator 44-40163 was a burned out hulk on the floor of the Baltic Sea.

• • •

"Bottle Baby," was lost on the Politz mission. The pilot, Lt. Milton Goodridge, was the sole survivor. (USAF)

CHAPTER 12
Third Mission
May 23, 1944

Our third mission was to an airfield in Avord, France. It was a milk run, no fighters and some flak. We dropped incendiaries. The right front bomb rack hung up. We unloaded three of the four bays. Pete elected to continue home. When we were over the Channel he had the bombardier manually release the incendiaries. He first alerted the other aircraft in the formation to stay away from us so they wouldn't get hit by them. We reported this to the Armaments Section. They later reported that changing the rack resolved the problem.

COMMENTARY

The airfield at Avord, which is still in operation, is located fifty miles south of Paris. The reason for attacking it becomes clear when you realize that the D-Day invasion took place only two weeks later on June 6. German aircraft flying from Avord could have easily attacked the Normandy beaches. In preparation for the landings, on this one day, the Eighth Air Force sent out 1,045 bombers and 1,206 fighters. That is an incredible feat by any standard. For its part, the 492nd BG put up 30 aircraft.

Dad brushes off this mission as a "milk run" with "some flak." The term "milk run" was given to short missions where no enemy opposition was encountered. Of course, anytime aircraft, especially large aircraft, are flying in close formation there is an element of danger. The process of assembling the attacking force, climbing to altitude, often in overcast weather, meant that mid-air collisions were not uncommon. Diaries written at the time by Lt. Bill Sparks (Crew 614) and S/Sgt Duane Heath (Crew 907) describe 45 minutes of heavy and accurate flak encountered during this mission. It might have been heavy but it was a good day for the 492nd. The group suffered no aircraft losses or casualties. The bomb rack problem will surface again. Val Preda was wise to alert other aircraft of their plan to manually release the bombs from the defective rack. Though uncommon, there were accounts of aircraft being struck by errant bombs.

• • •

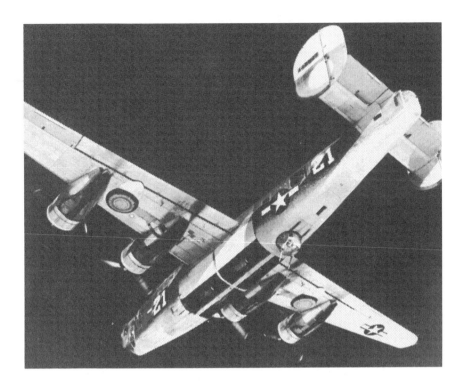

This Liberator is about to drop its lethal cargo. The catwalk between
the forward and aft crew compartments is visible between
the left and right bomb bays. (USAF)

CHAPTER 13
Fourth Mission
May 28, 1944

Our next mission was to an oil facility in Zeitz, Germany. Our bomb rack problem was not corrected as we found out when it was time to drop. May 28 began like any other day in a crewman's life. We were called about 11 P.M. and shaved, washed, and dressed. We went to the mess hall for our ritual breakfast of real eggs, toast, cereal, milk, coffee, and juice. Then we went to our lockers and put on our heated flight suits. The main briefing was at 1 A.M. When that was concluded pilots, navigators, bombardiers, and radio operators went to other briefings. We remaining crewmen went out to the aircraft. We had specific things to do there. I assisted the crew chief with ground run of the engines and other systems. Gunners checked their guns and ammo. After completion of ground checks I serviced the aircraft with 2750 gallons of high octane fuel. The last thing I checked was my upper turret for operation and ammo. Now we could relax, smoke a cigarette, and gab. The rest of the crew came back from their briefings and began checking the bombsight, navigation equipment, and radios. Pete checked the Form 1A maintenance record with me and the crew chief.

A flare went up signaled that it was time to saddle up. Everyone boarded the aircraft and went to their assigned positions. The next flare signaled us to start engines. Pete did another run up of the engines for his own satisfaction. The signal to taxi to the takeoff position was next. We were the lead aircraft on this mission so we started out first. As we waited at the end of the runway the signal was given and we started rolling forward. After a smooth takeoff, the others followed us at thirty-second intervals.

Pete flew a predetermined pattern. At 5,000 to 6,000 feet I started firing the flare gun with green flares. Each squadron had a different color to aid in assembling the formation. Assembly was completed as we headed toward France. I completed the fuel transfer, belted into my turret, and watched the formation line up behind us. The flight over the French coast was uneventful, no flak, no fighters.

When we reached the IP (initial point) our bombardier, Lt. Juan Rodriguez, told Pete he was having trouble with the bombsight. Pete contacted the deputy lead pilot who flew off our right wing. Pete instructed him to take over as the lead and we would drop on his signal. The next moments were very hairy. Our deputy lead pilot thought he was to take over our position in the formation. He dropped down, slid under us, and started coming back up. At the last possible second Pete spotted him and pulled up. He told the deputy to get back in position, and just pull straight ahead to form a left element. Everyone else stayed in their original positions. A mid-air collision was avoided. I heard that Pete really reamed this man out upon our return to base.

Now we were settled into our bombing formation. I swung my turret forward to see what was ahead of us. Off in the distance I could see B-17s as they were leaving the target area. They were late and we were on time. This is the time a pilot earns his keep. Pete's decision was to stay on our course, hoping the B-17s would be out of the way by the time we arrived over the target. Unfortunately, they hadn't cleared, so the scene over Zeitz was the intermeshing of two bomb groups as we continued to our assigned target. Fortunately there were no collisions but a number of near misses. We dropped our bombs and made our way home. Once on the ground we talked of our two near misses and agreed we were very lucky. Another mission had been completed.

COMMENTARY

The problem the crew had with the bomb rack on May 23 had returned. This must have been frustrating for the maintenance men who had replaced the rack five days earlier. Between these two missions Lt. Kehoe (Crew 613) flew this aircraft on Mission 9 to Belfort, France on May 25. It is not known whether they encountered any problem with the bomb rack.

When Lt. Rodriguez reported trouble with the bombsight you see that it was prudent to also have one in the deputy lead aircraft. Once on the bomb run the pilot handed over control of the aircraft to the bombardier. From this point on, until he called out "bombs away," the bombardier flew the airplane. He did this by means of the famous Norden bombsight. This complex device was wired into the auto-pilot and gave control signals that kept the plane on course to the target. When the bombsight calculated the precise point to put the bombs on the target it automatically dropped them.

The crew had a personnel change on this mission. The co-pilot for their first three missions, Lt. Elvern Seitzinger, was promoted to pilot in command of Crew 616. The crew's original pilot, Lt. James Kuntz, was injured in a fall from the wing of his aircraft during a post-flight inspection. By the time he returned to flight status the 492nd had been disbanded and he joined another unit.

When Pete Val Preda died in 1995 Dad wrote a letter of condolence to his family. In the letter Dad reminisced about some of the experiences he and Pete shared. He wrote that he couldn't remember the name of the co-pilot on the Zeitz mission. But he did remember that the co-pilot came back a nervous wreck. The two near collisions probably had something to do with it. He was sent to a rest home, what was called a "flack shack" for some rest and relaxation.

Coinciding with the arrival of the 492nd, the Eighth Air Force began a campaign against the German fuel and oil industry. This was the second time the 492nd had attacked Zeitz. On May 12 the group was part of a force that unleashed 250 tons of bombs on the city's synthetic oil facility, which converted coal into gasoline.

Adolf Hitler's armaments minister, Albert Speer, realized the impact of these attacks on Germany's ability to wage war. After the first Zeitz mission he wrote, "A new era in the air war began. It meant the end of German Armaments production." Speer visited the plant after the initial bombing. Production of fuel was reduced but not stopped. After 16 days of intensive repairs the facility was back up to full production. The Germans ability to repair these facilities had surprised even themselves. But on the 16th day, May 28, Crew 601 and their brothers-in-arms dropped another 450 tons of destruction on Zeitz, severely reducing production again. The bombing campaign against the synthetic oil plants took its toll. For the next eleven months, culminating with Germany's surrender, production of fuel was on a downward spiral. No other factor had such a negative impact on German war fighting capability.

Dispatching an aerial armada of over 2,000 bombers and fighters to do battle with the Axis was a monumental task. The Eighth Air Force accomplished this logistical and organizational marvel day after day. Consider that each four-engine bomber burns over 200 gallons of fuel per hour. Two thousand of them flying eight to 10 hours consumed gasoline at a rate of millions of gallons per day. The planners also had a multitude of variables to take into consideration, not the least of which was the abysmal English weather. As the bombers took off in thirty second intervals and climbed out through overcast skies, mid-air collisions were not uncommon. The flight characteristics of the various aircraft had to be taken into account: B-17s flew higher, but the B-24s flew faster. Escort fighters had limited flight time and fighter groups had to be sequenced in and out to provide maximum coverage. Missions to France were relatively short as compared to missions deep into the heart of Germany. Flight patterns had to be timed down to the minute to allow separation of outbound and inbound groups. They returned with battle damage to man and machine, and fuel tanks nearly empty.

The airspace over Zeitz was thick with bombers. Dad's description of the near collision of the 492nd and the B-17 group is a frightening account of how close they came to tragedy. When he recounts Val Preda's handling of the near miss caused by the pilot of the deputy lead aircraft, you can see that Dad's praise of Val Preda was not misplaced.

The last hurdle was that all these hundreds of airplanes were returning to a relatively small area of England. Many of them battle damaged and barely able to fly, many of them with dead and wounded aboard. Nothing better demonstrates the unrelenting efforts of the men of the Eighth Air Force than the fact that no matter how thick the flak, no matter how many fighters came up to do battle with them, no bomber group was ever diverted from its target due to enemy action.

Overall this was a good day for the 492nd BG, which suffered no losses. But other groups of the Eighth Air Force lost a total of 32 bombers.

• • •

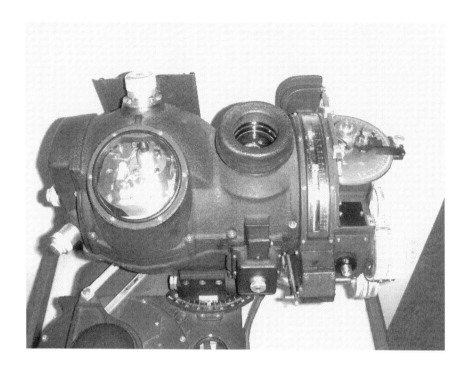

The famous Norden Bombsight was carried in each squadron's
lead aircraft. (Author)

CHAPTER 14
Fifth Mission
May 30, 1944

Our next mission was to bomb an air depot in Rotenburg, Germany. The first part of the mission was uneventful, but after leaving the target we were flying north to the Baltic Sea over Wilhelmshaven. The formation ahead of us was getting nailed with flak and we were going to fly along the same path. As we approached the flak concentration much of it was above us. We felt that the ones that exploded below were more of a problem. I heard things hit the aircraft, like a rain of nails, but nothing serious. We completed our run over Wilhelmshaven and out over the Baltic Sea. We turned west and headed for home. After landing we checked the aircraft for damage and found a single hole the size of a silver dollar in the outer wing panel. Our fifth mission was completed.

COMMENTARY

This mission occurred one week prior to D-Day. As the focus shifted to supporting the landings this was the last time the group would fly into Germany for the next three weeks. The 492nd Bomb Group dispatched 29 Liberators with Crew 601 taking the lead. Captain Wallace Hurley, the 856th Squadron Operations Officer, flew with them as Mission Command Pilot. Hurley was a very experienced pilot, having flown for an airline prior to the war. Two aircraft aborted the mission with mechanical problems. The remaining 27 aircraft dropped 67 tons of bombs on the target.

Dad describes flying through a flak barrage. A direct hit was not necessary as the exploding shells would throw out deadly shards of metal in all directions. Whereas the gunners could shoot back at enemy fighters, nothing could be done against the superb German 88 millimeter flak gun but tough it out and fly on. Herschel Smith, the pilot of Crew 906, confirmed Dad's statement that flak exploding below the aircraft was more lethal than flak exploding above it. Smith commented that the explosive energy of the shell is blasted upward.

Unbeknownst to the crew, they would only be together for three more weeks. Up to that final mission, the minor flak hole in the wing of the aircraft was the only damage the crew suffered to enemy action.

• • •

CHAPTER 15
Sixth Mission
June 10, 1944

Our sixth mission was to Boulogne, France. The target was coastal battery pill boxes. We carried four 2,000 pound bombs. On this was the mission I made a serious blunder. We were supposed to fly at 15,000 feet with an air temperature of 38 degrees. The time over the target was to be short, but all that turned out to be wrong. I wore long johns, regular outerwear, fur lined boots over black RAF shoes, and a leather helmet. As we took off everything was normal. We were the deputy lead. As the formation was assembled we crossed the Channel at 12,000 to 15,000 feet. We started to create contrails. A large formation produces large amount of these man-made clouds. Between the contrails and cloud cover aircraft were losing visual contact with each other. The lead ship continued to fly higher. We tried to maintain the formation but it became increasingly more difficult. We finally broke through the cloud layers at 20,000 feet. Val Preda was trying to get back into position. In the end we became the tail-end Charlie. Checking the number of aircraft that made it so far, one was missing. (Note: one 856th aircraft had aborted the mission with an overheated engine.) We went on with the mission.

Because of the cloud cover we were now following a pathfinder radar aircraft. The outside temperature was now -38 degrees. I started to feel tingling in my body, especially in my feet. After dropping our bombs we turned west and headed for home. I dropped from my turret and took off my boots and shoes. My socks were soaking wet and feet were bone white. On this mission we had a Command Pilot with us. Major Robert Hambaugh was the Squadron Commander of the 858th. He massaged one of my feet and I did the other. Val Preda got permission to leave the formation as we were over the Channel by this time. He turned on the heaters and the Major and I continued to massage my feet by the heater outlet. As we reached the base my feet were OK. I was able to put my boots on as we were landing. I swore I wouldn't do a stupid thing like that again. I wore my heated flying suit no matter what temperature was predicted. Our sixth mission was completed.

COMMENTARY

The 492nd flew two missions on June 10. Both were to bomb German-held airfields in France, not pillboxes as Dad stated. Dad's section of 24 Liberators, with one aborting the mission, bombed the airfield at Boulogne. Thirteen others bombed the airfield at Bricy. This was only four days after the D-Day landings and total air superiority was necessary for them to be successful. The group did well as they put their bombs on target and neither section suffered any casualties.

This five-hour mission to the coast of France was relatively short in contrast to the nine hour-round trip to Mulhouse a month before. This allowed for the maximum bomb load of four tons to be carried. The bomb bay was divided into forward and aft, left and right sections and a two thousand pound bomb could be carried in each.

The crew's silver airplane, 44-40163, was not available and for the second time they flew a mission in the olive drab "Little Lulu." Both aircraft were destroyed 10 days later.

Dad made a mistake by assuming that the mission would be flown at a lower and warmer altitude. At 20,000 feet, temperatures routinely fall to -30 degrees Fahrenheit. In that extreme cold heated flying suits are a necessity. The official name of the clothing is the F-2 Flying Suit Assembly. The basic components are a jacket, trousers, and boots. Each is worn over a liner embedded with heating wires similar to an electric blanket. The suit was plugged into a 24-volt direct current electrical receptacle located at each crew station. Dad was wearing his F-2 flying suit when he was shot down. Without the liner, the jacket is not very heavy, but it was his only overcoat through the cold German winter of 1944-45. We have the jacket to this day and it is a family treasure.

Major Robert Hambaugh was one of the only combat veterans when the 492nd arrived in England. He had won a Silver Star as the pilot of a Douglas A-24 dive bomber in the Pacific Theater. One week after this mission was flown Hambaugh's command, the 858th Bomb Squadron, was dissolved and the 492nd became a three-squadron group. Hambaugh was sent to the Eighth Air Force base at Cheddington and assumed command of the 36th Bomb Squadron. The 36th was unique in that its B-24s carried no bombs into combat. Instead, powerful electronic equipment in their bomb bays jammed the radar systems that aimed the German flak batteries.

CHAPTER 16
Seventh Mission
June 14, 1944

Our seventh mission was to Emmerich, Germany. This was a classic milk run, no fighters and some flak. We were in and out in easy fashion. The return to base was uneventful.

COMMENTARY

The 492nd attacked two targets on this day. One was the oil refinery at Emmerich, Germany. The other was the airfield at Chateaudun, France. There is a question of which target Crew 601 hit. Dad remembers bombing Emmerich but all of my research points to Chateaudun. The 856th Squadron, which Crew 601 was part of, put up nine aircraft. Crew 616 aborted and the other eight attacked Chateaudun. The mission was led by the 856th Squadron Commander, Major Jack Losee. He flew with Crew 606.

According to the flight records, on the following day, the crew flew a two-hour non-combat flight. The purpose of this flight is not known. It was however, the last landing Crew 601 would ever make. The next time out – Politz and the veteran fighter pilots of the Luftwaffe!

• • •

"Little Lulu" leads the 856th Bomb Squadron. The silver B-24 behind it is Val Preda's unnamed 44-40163. (USAF)

CHAPTER 17
Eighth Mission
June 20, 1944

On June 17, 1944, I returned from a three-day pass in London. I was tired and sleepy. We had seen V-1 "buzz bombs" attacking the city. The V-1 was the cruise missile of its day. As they flew over, pedestrians and traffic came to a dead stop. When the pulse jet engine stopped, the V-1 plummeted to earth. There was a loud explosion—then everything resumed like nothing happened.

While relaxing in our hut, we were informed we were scheduled to fly the next day. This was a last-minute substitution as we were not scheduled to fly this mission. The normal procedure was to have one day off after returning from a three-day pass. Captain Peter Val Preda gave us enlisted men the final say. He said he and the other officers would abide by our decision to go or not to go. We talked it over and figured we were indestructible… We would go. It turned out to be a deadly decision, one we would all regret for the rest of our lives. For some of us, the rest of our lives were measured in decades, and for others, only in seconds.

We were awakened at 11 p.m. and went to the mess hall, then to the briefing hut. After briefing we went to our flight lockers, dressed in our combat outfits, received our escape kits, picked up our chutes and on to our aircraft. With the aircraft crew chief, we performed pre-flight inspection, ground run of the engines and accessories. After shutdown we serviced the aircraft with a full fuel load. When this was all completed I checked out my upper turret for operation and ammo load. The armorers loaded the bombs for the mission.

The only difference this day from other mission days was we were snapping at each other, like a premonition this was not going to be an easy mission. We were waiting for the pilot, co-pilot, navigators, and bombardier so we stood around by our lonesome selves smoking, thinking, and waiting for load-up and taxi-out. I felt once we started to move everything would fall into place, our thoughts would be on other things. When everyone was together we wished each other good luck, entered the aircraft into our respective positions waiting for the flare from the operations to start engines. Another flare signaled taxi into take-off sequence.

Our position was deputy lead to Lt. Nicholas Kehoe. After take-off we assembled into a three-squadron group. During assembly Val Preda informed me he lost turbo power to number one engine. I replaced the turbo amplifier with the spare. Pete increased power setting and the amplifier failed while the group assembly was going on. I crisscrossed the discriminator tubes between the two units. After a couple changes the amplifier came on line and turbo power was restored to the number one engine.

My next task was to transfer fuel from auxiliary tanks to the mains. We were over the Channel in formation when the fuel transfer was completed. After getting set in my turret, I noticed the group was in close formation and reported this to Pete. Approaching Helgoland Island, Germany a strong flak center, Lt. Kehoe made a shift away from the island resulting in the spreading of our group. Reaching the Baltic Sea the formation was still trying to come together. I informed Pete we were still not tight as a formation should be. I don't know if he called Lt. Kehoe to inform him of our formation.

Before we reached Rugen Island, and because of cold temperatures, Val Preda called on the gunners to test fire their guns. Not long after this while traversing my turret, I stopped, looking aft, I saw what looked like flak explosions and remarked that someone was catching flak. With my next breath I called out, "Enemy fighters six o'clock low!" Then all hell broke loose. Messerschmitt 410 (Me-410) fighters hit us from all sides. We had RAF P-51s flying cover for us. This action took place as soon as they left us to cover aircraft coming out of the flak areas. German fighters usually waited for bomber cripples.

Aircraft behind and above were falling out of the sky. The 410s were having a field day. One 410 came alongside the left waist window. No one was firing from the waist position. The 410 then moved forward and up. Now my guns were able to fire. I began firing, scoring hits but the 410 just dropped below my wing. The gun interrupters cut in and my guns stopped firing. The 410 then dropped further and fell back below our tail section and began firing his 20mm cannons into the rear of our aircraft. Explosions in the waist area were followed by explosions and a fireball in the bomb bay. We were carrying fifty-two, 100 pound bombs. The next explosion was in the flight deck at Walt Kean's radio operator's position. He was hit in the right leg.

Then our aircraft began spinning and going down. The force of the spin caused my seat latches to release and I fell to the deck next to Walt's leg! We looked at each other and thought this is what it's like to die! Somehow Val Preda regained control and got us out of the death spiral we were in. I entered the bomb bay and saw fire all around the bombs. I opened the bomb bay doors. The blast of air blew the flames away from the bombs. The command deck, where the oxygen bottles were stored, was blown apart. The escaping oxygen fanned the flames and the aft bomb bay was ablaze. The hydraulic tank was hit and the oil poured out, adding more fuel to the fire. Kean was moving toward the bomb bay. I hooked a static line to his parachute harness and threw him out.

Meanwhile, Val Preda was losing speed because he was using the engines for flight control. He tried the auto pilot and would get all the lights on, but when he hit the master switch, the aircraft would begin to roll. He turned off the switch, tried it again and got the same result. At this point he told me to get the navigators. We carried two on this mission, Lt. Rudie Bartel and Lt. John Saul. The bombardier, Lt. Juan Rodriguez, had already bailed out. As Bartel passed me, he remarked we were 20 miles south of Sweden. "Great," I said, I told him I was going back to fight the fire. The fire was like a blow torch, oxygen under pressure and hydraulic oil feeding it. My seven-pound extinguisher was quickly emptied. The aluminum nearest the fire was running down like water. The access door to the waist position was partially open. It just moved a little. It was jammed. I called through the opening. Bending down, I could see someone who appeared to be hanging by his harness. I believe it was Staff Sergeant Miles Toepper. I called again and then I threw the fire extinguisher through the opening, trying to get someone, anyone… no response.

As I headed forward I noticed the two navigators were gone and the co-pilot, Lt. Walton, was sitting on the catwalk. As I approached him I told him to jump, which he did. I moved forward again but stopped because Val Preda was now standing in front of me. I told him I didn't have my chute on and for him to jump. As I cleared the bomb racks I put my chest pack on and bailed out. I was the last man out. Hitting the slipstream, I tumbled many times. Suddenly everything seemed to stop. I felt like I was motionless. It was so calm and smooth it almost made me believe I was not falling. Realizing it was time to pull my ripcord… in my haste to bail out, I had put my pack on backwards. Grabbing with my right hand, no cord, looked down, saw it was on the left side. I pulled the cord, watched my chute deploy into a beautiful mushroom. Then there was a very hard jolt, slowing me from 120 MPH to approximately 25 MPH. I was glad my harness was on tight and snug. My body absorbed the shock without effects.

As I was coming down I heard a loud roar, looked up and saw my plane's wing go by, just missing the chute. The number two fuel tank was on fire. I watched it as it continued to spiral and crash into the Pomeranian Bay and burst into flames. Suddenly it was time to unfasten my harness in preparation of hitting the water. I only released one latch before I hit the water going backwards. I tried to spin the chute so I could land falling forward without success. I was hovering directly above the burning aircraft. Fortunately a surface wind drifted me away from the fire landing about 75 to 100 feet from the burning aircraft.

I quickly unhooked the remaining latches, inflated my life vest, and proceeded to swim away from the aircraft. My life vest had not been modified, the neck portion pushing my head into the water... very cold water. Whatever currents were present prevented me from getting away from the burning aircraft. I became waterlogged, cold and my "Lil' Abner" heated shoes were dragging me down like cement blocks. I thought I was going to sleep with the fishes.

A German crash boat from the seaplane base kept circling the crash site, as well as me. Finally, I whistled to attract their attention. Very cautiously they approached me, grabbed me, and sped away. One of the crew spoke English. He told me to remove my clothes; he spread them on the deck to dry. I was blue from the water. Standing in shorts under the June sun my body warmed up and the blue color vanished. This same crewman took my cigarettes, broke them apart and spread them on the deck. As sections dried he would gather a clump and with cigarette paper roll me a cigarette. Very pleasant, inhaling added warmth to my insides.

The Germans were curious about the objects floating in the water. I told them they were oxygen bottles and they were relieved because they though they were bombs. My watch stopped at 9:25. We cruised around long enough for my clothes to dry before we headed for shore. We put in at the seaplane base. I walked up the dock with all dry clothes wondering what lay ahead. All personal effects were removed. When the officer saw a box of matches the crewman gave me for the tobacco, he wanted to know where I got it. When I told him it seemed to satisfy him. All of *the tobacco was taken as well as the matches. We spent the night at the seaplane base. Our lives as POWs had begun!*

COMMENTARY

During his three-day pass to London, Dad witnessed the damage done by the some of the first V-1 "buzz bombs" to hit the city. They were given that nickname by war-weary Londoners for the distinctive sound of the unique pulse jet engine. Ten thousand were launched from sites in northern France and aimed at London. Twenty four hundred hit the city. The V-1 was fired from a catapult in the direction of the target. The simple autopilot kept the missile on its flight path. When a propeller-driven counter mounted on the nose reached a predetermined limit, the engine shut off and the control surfaces put the V-1 into a steep dive. The 1,900-pound warhead exploded on impact. The lack of pinpoint accuracy meant the V-1 would most effectively be fired at large population centers. Dad describes the reaction of the British people to these attacks as being quite matter of fact, almost indifferent. But they had been through this before. The German bombing of London, called the blitz, killed 43,000 British civilians from September of 1940 to May of 1941. The death toll from the V-1 was to add another 6,000. There was a very small window of opportunity for Dad to have seen any V-1 attacks. The first of them were fired at London on June 13 and Dad's pass began four days later. Only one week after the first V-1 struck London he was being led through the streets of Stralslund, Germany, on his way to a POW camp, never to see England again.

This was the eighth and final mission of Crew 601. The group dispatched 35 aircraft to the synthetic oil production facility in Politz, on the German-Polish border. The area was heavily defended but disrupting the flow of fuel to the Axis war machine was of vital importance. It was the second time the 492nd had hit that target. The first time was Mission 12 on May 29 when three aircraft were lost. This time the toll was to be much higher.

The fact that the Crew 601 was not scheduled to fly this mission may have been due to illness on the part of Lt. Orrin Bowland, the pilot of replacement Crew R-11. As a result, Val Preda was called on to fly the mission. Five of Bowland's men flew with other crews on that fateful day. But none of them returned to North Pickenham, all were

75

shot down. Three were taken prisoner, and two were killed in action. Bowland's co-pilot, Lt. Cary Walton, flew with Crew 601 as Pete Val Preda's co-pilot.

The deadly decision of the enlisted men on the crew to fly the mission when they didn't have to was probably due not just to feeling, as Dad says, "indestructible," but to also feeling they were a lucky crew. On the first seven missions Crew 601 flew, two aircraft had been lost. But neither was lost to enemy action, both had run out of fuel while returning from the mission to Mulhouse, France. One man was killed and the other nine were injured, three so badly that they were sent back to the States to recover. There were no losses at all on the crew's next six missions. They may also have believed the mission would be relatively easy—yet another "milk run." Since the beginning of June the group had flown 19 missions. Seventeen of them were of a tactical nature in the vicinity of Normandy, the scene of the D-Day landings which took place on the sixth of June. Four aircraft were lost on three of those missions. The group had bombed German soil on only two occasions, Mission 26 to the oil refinery at Emmerich on June 14, and Mission 31 to the airfield at Luneberg on the June 18.

A second deadly decision was made that day. Although S/Sgt Jack Reed flew as a waist gunner, he had been trained as a flight engineer. As such he was Dad's assistant. Reed had expressed to Dad his desire to fly some missions "up front" as the engineer. He and Dad agreed to trade positions on this mission. Possibly due to the fact that the crew was not originally slated to fly this mission, or simply force of habit, Dad did his normal preflight inspection of the aircraft and the men took their usual stations. At the time, putting off the change must have seemed insignificant. But it was to have a profound impact. All four of the gunners in the rear of the aircraft were killed. If the change had been made, Jack Reed could have survived and returned to his family in Arkansas. As for our family, my mother would have been a widow and I would have been another "Gold Star Kid" of the 492nd.

As the group was assembling, the failure of the number one engine turbocharger was a critical problem. The turbocharger pressurizes the engine's air fuel mixture, making up for the increasingly thinner air as the aircraft climbs. Dad successfully determined the cause to be a faulty amplifier which controlled the operation of the turbocharger. If he had been unsuccessful in making the repairs, Val

Preda would not have been able to keep up with the formation. He would have been forced to abort the mission and return to base. Crew 601 would have survived the infamous Mission 34.

The table of organization for a military organization begins with a single entity at the top and breaks down into progressively smaller units. The Eighth Air Force was made up of three air divisions. The Second Air Division was had five combat wings with three bomb groups in each. Typically, the Wings flew one behind the other. The 14th Combat Wing was under the command of General Leon Johnson. For the Politz mission the Wing's three groups were arranged in a triangular formation. In the lead was the 44th Bomb Group. Flying behind and to the right was the 392nd and to the left was the 492nd. Each group was further divided into three sections: a lead section, a high right section, and a low left section. In the case of the 492nd, the high right section had 11 aircraft, and the lead and low left sections had 12 aircraft. The 856th Squadron flew in the low left section. It was arranged in four, three-ship elements. The lead element flew ahead of the other three elements, which flew behind the leader in a line abreast of each other. Each element had a leader who flew in front with a left and right wingman flying slightly behind.

The front element was comprised of the lead aircraft flown by Lt. Nick Kehoe (Crew 613), in "Flak Happy." To the left was Lt. Eugene Hadden (Crew 608), flying "Little Lulu." The deputy lead, Captain Pete Val Preda (Crew 601), was Kehoe's right wingman in 44-40163. As section lead and deputy lead, Kehoe and Val Preda each had an extra navigator aboard. This made for a total of 11 aboard rather than the usual 10-man crew.

Directly behind the lead element was an element led by Val Preda's former co-pilot Lt. Elvern Seitzinger (Crew 616), flying "SKNAP-PY." Seitzinger's wingmen were Lt. Roscoe Harris (Crew 612) in "Four Beers Doc," and Lt. Richard Kaufman (Crew R-05) in "Troublehunter."

On Seitzinger's left was the element led by Flight Officer Armando Velarde (Crew 615) in "Tabasco Keeds." His left wingman was Lt. Milton Goodridge (Crew 812) in "Bottle Baby." The Goodridge crew had been assigned to the 858th Squadron but that organization had been disbanded the day before. The 858th crews and aircraft were then assigned to other squadrons, with the Goodridge crew going to the

856th. Velarde's right wingman was Lt. George McKoy (Crew R-09) in the "Ruptured Duck."

On Seitzinger's right was the element lead by Lt. John Curtis (Crew 610) in his aircraft "The Mary Ellen." His wingmen were Lt. George Faucher (Crew R-12) in "The Lady Will" and Lt. Franklin Abbot (Crew 609) in 44-40128. In all, 119 men were aboard the 12 Liberators of the 856th Bomb Squadron as they left England on the morning of June 20, 1944.

The group assembled and began climbing out over the North Sea. Dad states that the formation started to spread apart as they flew over Helgoland, an island west of Denmark. This did not bode well. The key to maximizing the effectiveness of the bombers' defensive armament is to maintain a tight formation.

They crossed the Danish peninsula and droned on over the Baltic Sea, Velarde's aircraft developed a turbocharger problem on the number two engine. To compensate for the loss of power on number two, Velarde increased power on number one. The extra demand placed on that engine resulted in its failure. At that point he opted to abort the mission. He was less than 100 miles from the coast of Sweden, where he and his crew could have spent the remainder of the war as internees. Instead, he chose to take his crippled ship over 500 miles back to England on two good engines and one at reduced power. Although they would have been an enticing target for Luftwaffe fighters, they successfully evaded them and hours later touched down on the runway at North Pickenham. The other 11 aircraft and 109 men of the 856th continued on.

The P-51 escort fighters Dad had seen were not from the Royal Air Force, but were American, from the 339th Fighter Group. As the 339th left the area due to low fuel, their replacements from the 355th Fighter Group were late in coming on the scene. They were having problems jettisoning a new type of drop tank they had recently been equipped with. Dropping the external fuel tanks was necessary for the fighters to be maneuverable enough to take on German interceptors. The gap in fighter protection was only four minutes long, but it could not have come at a worse time.

Shortly after Velarde turned back the formation made a right turn. The new heading put it on a straight course to the target. From its position on the left of the formation, the 856th was on the outside of the turn. They had to cover more ground than the right section and they fell behind. This did not go unnoticed by those in the other sections. Lt. Charles Bastien (Crew 714) describes looking out his window and being "shocked to see the Low Left Squadron lagging way back several hundred yards, and alone: it was terribly wrong!!!"

It also didn't go unnoticed by the Luftwaffe. The veteran fliers of Zerstorergeschwader 26, a bomber destroyer squadron, seized the opportunity and attacked. Most accounts agree that a force of thirty-five Me-410 Hornisse (Hornet) aircraft pounced on the low left section. The Hornet was a large twin-engine fighter, armed with machine guns, cannons, and rockets, all of which they unleashed on the exposed Liberators of the 856th Squadron.

The speed of the attack shocked those who witnessed it. T/Sgt Jim McCrory was "Herk" Taylor's radio operator on Crew R-04. From his vantage point at the rear of the lead section, McCrory described the lightning attack as taking "approximately 30 seconds." Waist gunner Sgt. Scott Hilliard of the 446th Bomb Group was flying right behind the 492nd. He describes the B-24s of the 856th Squadron as "lighting up like Christmas trees and going down. They were there one minute and gone the next." Hilliard took several photos with a K-20 camera from his position. He took a haunting photo of the bay south of Rugen Island. Five plumes of smoke rise from the water, evidence of the fate of five of the nine bombers.

When the German fighters made their destructive pass through the formation Kehoe's aircraft took a great many hits and caught fire. Not expecting the flaming craft to make it, the rest of the crew bailed out. Kehoe was able to engage the autopilot and check on the progress of the fire. Using an extinguisher he was able to put it out. He returned to the pilot's seat and set a course for Sweden. When the aircraft reached Sweden, Kehoe knew it was too badly damaged to attempt a landing. He bailed out and was interned for the remainder of the war. Kehoe's navigator, Lt. Milton Grossman, and his waist gunner, Sgt. Lanta Redmond, were captured by the Germans. The remaining eight men did not survive.

After the ME-410s made their fierce attack through the formation, Seitzinger realized that he and Kehoe were the only squadron mates still flying. With fuel leaking at a prodigious rate, "SKNAPPY" set a course for Sweden. Swedish fighter planes escorted them to Malmo

Airfield. Seitzinger landed his damaged craft and the ten-man crew was interned for the remainder of the war.

The Hadden crew in the olive drab "Little Lulu" went down with all hands. Among them was Lt. Luke Rybarczyk, Val Preda's original bombardier.

A rocket hit the left wing of "Bottle Baby" severing it. The stricken bomber rolled over and exploded. Its pilot, Lt. Goodridge, was blown out of the airplane. He was the only survivor.

S/Sgt Robert Cash, Lt. McKoy's radio operator on the "Ruptured Duck," was the sole survivor of the nine-man crew. Their navigator, Lt. John Saul, had been assigned to Val Preda's crew for the mission.

"Four Beers Doc" went down with seven KIA, among them its pilot Lt. Harris. T/Sgt Vincent Muscarnera met up with fellow crewman S/Sgt Dallas Thomas at Stalag Luft IV and found out that their bombardier, Lt. Herbert Wisner, also survived.

Lt. Kaufman and the crew of "Troublehunter" went down with all hands. The body of the bombardier, Lt. Robert Zipfel, was the only one ever recovered.

Lt. Faucher and six of his crew from "The Lady Will" were taken prisoner. Three men were killed, two during the attack and one drowned after bailing out.

"The Mary Ellen" took a direct hit in the fuel tanks. Lt. Terry Diggs, Faucher's co-pilot, recalled that the first sign they were under attack was "a huge ball of fire where Curtis had been." The Curtis crew never had a chance.

Lt. Abbot and the ten-man crew of 44-40128 were all killed when their Liberator exploded. The body of Sgt. Dennis Kent, a waist gunner, was the only one ever recovered.

The results of the day's operation were disastrous. The 856th was wiped out. Of the 12 aircraft that left North Pickenham that morning, "Tabasco Keeds" was the only one to return to fight another day. Of the rest, 77 were killed, 21 were taken prisoner, and 11 were interned in Sweden. Two of the POWs later died in captivity.

Four of the KIA and seven POW were from Crew 601. When Walt Kean was struck in the right leg by a 20mm shell the impact severed the limb. By hooking Kean's ripcord to a static line and pushing him out of the bomb bay Dad saved his life. The static line deployed the parachute automatically, something Kean could not have done if

he had lost consciousness. Once on the ground, Kean was broug.
to a German doctor who did his best to save Kean's life. The doctor dressed his wounds and contacted the authorities. Because of his
wounds Kean was declared a "liability" by the German government. A
liability was defined as someone who would detract from the Allied
war effort if sent home. As such he was not sent to a POW camp but
was repatriated. He was returned to the United States aboard the
U.S.S. Gripsholm, a hospital ship operated by the Red Cross.

For every aircraft lost in combat a Missing Air Crew Report was
generated. In the case of Crew 601 it is MACR 7080. The report is a
collection of pertinent information on the aircraft and crew. Some
of the information is official such as equipment serial numbers, etc.
There is also a list of the next of kin. Much of the report seeks to de-
termine what happened to every member of the crew. After the war
three of the seven survivors were interviewed. The respondents were
Rudie Bartel, Carey Walton, and Walt Kean. Each answered a Casualty
Questionnaire. In the CQ the men give an account of what happened
to them and the other survivors. Accompanying each one is a set of
four Individual Casualty Questionnaires. In these the respondent tells
what he knows about the fate of each man who was killed.

Along with the three questionnaires we have two other accounts.
One, of course, is Dad's description of the mission. Another is Pete Val
Preda's, which he gave to author Robert Laird. Of these five accounts,
four are consistent in their observations. Val Preda simply states that
the four gunners were killed but doesn't go into detail. Dad looked
through the jammed access door into the rear of the aircraft. He saw
someone hanging by his harness but was unable to get a response
from anyone.

Bartel and Walton stated that the gunners were last seen as they
entered the aircraft and last heard over the intercom about one half
hour before the attack. Walton added, "My supposition is that they
were killed in the fierce air attack but if any jumped he drowned before he was picked up".

That consensus would seem to be the end of it. But then we come
to Kean's ICQ accounts. They are very different and in conflict with
the other four. He stated that he saw Toepper and Reed attempting
to give first aid to St. Pierre and Pierce! He claimed Pierce was last
seen "lying on the deck next to the ball turret after being removed

from the turret by Reed and Toepper." He goes on to say that St. Pierre was "seen lying on the floor of aircraft over the rear escape hatch." He comments on St. Pierre, "I am sure that this man is dead. Reed signaled to me that he was fatally injured." In light of Kean's injuries the information is surprising to say the least. He had to be hooked up to a static line and pushed out of the airplane. He said two men bailed out before he did, most likely Rodriguez and Saul. After he bailed out he saw two men come out of the waist window who he believed to be Reed and Toepper. He added, "Pilot Val Preda and engineer Centore attempting to control aircraft". In any case, it's hard to believe that Kean had the opportunity, or for that matter the ability, to see what was happening back in the waist area.

Dad had the utmost respect for Pete Val Preda both as an officer and as a pilot. In his letter of condolence to Pete's family he wrote, "From where I stand – I would not be writing this letter if not for your Dad's great flying ability. For that I'm thankful and honored to have been a member of his crew". If Val Preda could not have gotten the aircraft out of the death spin they would have found themselves pinned against the walls of the fuselage, fighting vainly against the increasing centrifugal force as the spiral tightened. With all hope gone, they would have ridden the burning craft to their deaths.

Along with the annihilation of the 856th Squadron the group also lost three aircraft from the 857th Squadron. Major John Losee was in command of the mission and flying with Lt. Joe Harris (Crew 707) in the "Silver Witch." They were hit by flak as they flew over the target. It looked like they were going down. The navigator, Lt. James Sconyers, bailed out and fell into enemy hands. Harris and his co-pilot Lt. Harold Burkhalter found that with great difficulty they could control the ship. They were able to make it to Sweden where the crew was interned.

Lt. Malcolm Heber (Crew 705) in "Say When" lost the number four engine to flak damage. They were struck by two bombs dropped from aircraft above them. Luckily the bombs did not explode but the extensive damage ruled out a return to England. "Say When" made it to Sweden and the crew was interned.

Lt. Robert Liggett (Crew 701) in 44-40106 was damaged by German fighters inbound to the target. They dropped their bombs and left the formation en route to Sweden, the fourth 492nd aircraft to do so. In total, seventeen B-24s found refuge in Sweden from the force that attacked Politz.

T/Sgt Gildo Gregori was the flight engineer for Lt. Dave O'Sullivan (Crew 713). He and the rest of the crew of the "Irishman's Shanty" had survived the first Politz mission in May. They would later become the first 492nd crew to complete a 30-mission tour. Gregori's diary entry for June 21 acknowledges the extent of the slaughter: "Yesterday my crew didn't fly but others did and only 18 crews returned out of 35 that took off... [We] lost nearly all the buddies that left with us from the States."

Although the group suffered its highest one-day losses, it was called on to do battle the very next day. On June 21 the 492nd scraped together eleven aircraft and flew Mission 35, a deep penetration into the heart of Germany. They bombed the aircraft engine plant at Genshagen. All 11 aircraft returned safely.

• • •

Thirty five Messerschmitt Me-410 Hornet fighters, such as this one, wreaked havoc on the 856th Bomb Squadron. (Ramsay Library, New England Air Museum)

CHAPTER 18
CAPTURED!
June 21, 1944

The next day the guards woke us up early and told us we would be leaving soon. After we cleaned ourselves as best we could we were given some black bread and some ersatz coffee. Our assigned guards, two young privates and an older sergeant took us from the seaplane base into the town of Stralsund. There were five of us, Val Preda, Walton, Bartel, Saul, and me. The town looked peaceful, quiet, and untouched by war. We passed a lone policeman. He was wearing a Prussian style hat and a green coat with silver buttons. His pants were gray with red stripes down the legs.

Arriving at the nearly deserted railroad station the people there ignored us, which was good. The sergeant kept us at the end of the platform away from everyone as we waited for the train. When it arrived the sergeant put us into a compartment big enough for the eight of us. I don't remember much about the ride except that the area we went through seemed untouched by the war. The sergeant told Bartel, who could speak some German, that we would be going to Berlin, change trains, and proceed to Frankfurt.

As we reached the outskirts of Berlin, air raid sirens started going off. The train stopped and we were told to stay in the compartment. The guards went outside and we heard the flak guns firing at our guys. We could see the 8th Air Force formations overhead. They flew though air thick with black smoke from the exploding shells. It was said that the flak over Berlin was thick enough to walk on. After seeing it from the ground I believe that wasn't too much of an exaggeration. We didn't see any of our planes fall from the sky. I hoped all of them made it back to their home bases.

Fortunately no bombs fell where we were. After the all clear siren blew I looked out the window and saw that we had stopped next to an elevated gun emplacement called a flak tower. How fortunate we were that it didn't attract the attention of any P-51 fighters who would seek out targets of opportunity for strafing runs.

At this point the guards returned to the compartment and the train slowly moved toward the station. The train stopped at the platform and we disembarked. As the guards led us through the station we saw a lot of bomb damage. Many people were wearing goggles and holding hand-kerchiefs over their mouths for protection from the thick dust in the air. We left the station and found a chaotic scene outside. Ambulances, fire engines, and trucks were speeding by. There was smoke, dust, fire and explosions and people running in all directions. It was total panic in the streets of Berlin that day.

In all this confusion the old sergeant was somehow able to comman-deer a truck to take us to a station on the other side of the city. But when we got there the sergeant found out that the station was closed due to bomb damage to the tracks. He started us walking through the streets of Berlin. Where we were going was the big question. Amid the confusion of the air raid we walked on the Unter Den Linden. We were accosted by elderly people calling us Roosevelt gangsters, Chicago gangsters, and terror fliegers (flyers). They were very vocal and agitated. Many of them spit at us. The sergeant sensed the crowd's malevolent nature. He told Bartel to tell the rest of us that if the angry crowd pulled anyone out for a summary execution, do not look back and just keep moving. As the only enlisted man I was the tail end Charlie and the most likely to be grabbed. I remember hoping that the crowd wouldn't get any madder than they already were. We kept moving and they eventually fell back. For the mo-ment the situation was defused. But the prospect of being lynched by that mob strikes a fear in me I can still feel to this day.

As we passed the Wilhelmstrasse we saw that the bombing had caused a great deal of damage. Many buildings were on fire. We walked for quite a while and came to a long red building about four stories high. We entered through a small door within a large door. The large door was used to allow vehicles to enter. Inside was a courtyard in which burning objects scattered throughout. The sergeant led us down a flight of stairs to a German Red Cross food kitchen. We were fed alfalfa soup, black bread, and ersatz coffee. After the meal we climbed the stairs to the top floor. We were locked up and our guards left. From our vantage point on the top floor we could look out across the city. We saw large columns of smoke. We heard secondary explosions and sirens.

Being very tired we lied down on the bunks. The mattresses were bur-lap sacks filled with excelsior, a stuffing made from wood shavings, and fell asleep. I don't remember how long we were there but I think it was the next day, June 22nd. When the sergeant came back I was completely refreshed, like I had slept the clock around. We left the building without another meal. We walked back to the station without incident. We stood at the end of the platform alone at first. Soon after civilians started coming in carrying suitcases and bundles of clothes. I believe they were leaving the city for safer areas.

Before long the platform was filled with people but fortunately no one bothered us. When the train arrived people were pushing, shoving, and yelling at each other. We knew we faced a problem. The refugees had taken all the compartments and we were standing in the aisles. The old sergeant came through. He confronted the woman conductor and a very vocal exchange took place between them. She went to the nearest compartment and made the people get out and stand in the aisle. We then were marched into the compartment past the standees. We received dirty looks and most likely some nasty remarks but we were safely installed in the compartment.

After an uneventful ride we arrived in Frankfurt. As we were walking through the terminal we heard our names called out. Looking around, we saw coming toward us our bombardier, Lt. Rodriguez. After greeting each other our four guards marched us out of the station and on the road to the Dulag Luft interrogation center. We were unshaven and dirty, and looked like gangsters. The people standing on the side of the road saw us in the worst light.

When we arrived at the Dulag Luft we were put into a room that resembled a walk-in refrigerator. They came for us one at a time starting with Captain Val Preda until all the officers were gone. I was now alone, waiting for my turn. Finally they came for me. I was taken to a room upstairs where a German officer was sitting at his desk. I saw cigarettes on the desk and asked if I could have one. He offered me one and gave me a light. The first few draws made my head swim but it gave my cold insides some warmth.

He began speaking to me in Italian. When I ignored what he said he asked in English, "Don't you know your mother's language?" I responded that I was an American. He said I was stupid for not knowing the mother tongue.

He put a form in front of me told me I had to fill it out so they could notify the Red Cross that I was a POW. I looked at the form. It asked for more than name, rank, and service number. It asked about my organization, etc. He even started to tell me about the 492nd Bomb Group. He knew when we arrived in England, where we were located, and the Commanding Officer's name. I gave him my name, rank, and service number. Thank God they had given us classes on what to do if captured. The interrogating officer's questions and threats were almost verbatim to the scenario described to us in England.

In the meantime I kept smoking his cigarettes and he kept pressuring me to fill out the form. So I filled out the name, rank, and service number and proceeded to draw cross lines over the rest of the form. He didn't like that and called a guard who took me out of the office to a room across the hall. I was joined by a young RAF airman. We looked at each other warily, not saying anything. The guard brought in two bowls of barley soup. I was given a USA mess kit with a rusty spoon. I didn't care, I was hungry. We ate in silence. As I was finishing I said, "Some grub", and he answered, "Yes it is". That was our total conversation. The guard returned and removed the bowls and utensils.

A short while later the guard returned. He took me to what was to be my isolation room. Before I entered the room the guard told me to remove my shoes. These were the same heated shoe liners I wore during all our walking and were still good. He said to place them by the door. If I needed to use the facilities a drawstring inside the room would raise an arrow outside and the guard would take me to the bathroom.

With these instructions I entered the world of isolation. The room measured approximately eight feet by eight feet. An opaque wire-reinforced window let in a little bit of daylight. There was one skimpy blanket, thank God it was summer. I lied down and immediately fell asleep.

After a few days, maybe three, I lost count; I was taken by a guard to an office outside the building. Another German officer started again to interrogate me. I gave him the same responses. While sitting at his desk I noticed a collage of the Normandy beachhead with line denoting the present positions of the Allied army. I inquired how the invasion was going. His response to me was, "If Eisenhower doesn't mess it up, you'll be home for Christmas". With that he dismissed me. I inquired about a shower and shave. He told the guard it was okay. He also gave me another cigarette. I saluted and left with the guard. The shower was cold water with a partially blocked shower head and a small piece of soap. The razor was a Gillette, double-edged and dull. I honed the blade inside a glass to improve the edge. I managed to get a decent shave and shower.

Now I felt more like myself – clean. The guard took me back to my isolation room. He gave me a soft cover book to read, probably taken from some GI. All I needed was a light for my cigarette and the guard didn't have any matches. He said to go down the hall to the next guard. Well, I wandered along the halls until I found a guard with a match. I was very close to the door to the outside but more guards were there so I gave up the idea of taking a walk in the sun. I returned to my room. I was clean, had a book to read, and was smoking a cigarette. Life had taken a turn for the better.

As usual it didn't last long. I had finished the smoke and was getting into the book; the title long since forgotten. A guard opened the door and told me to follow him. I was taken outside to another building where other POWs were staying. I was told to pick a bunk. I met Val Preda there, but don't remember seeing any other members of the crew. This area was for POWs who would be shipped out to Wetzlar, a transient camp.

The next day we left Dulag Luft early in the morning. I believe this was so the locals wouldn't see what we looked like cleaned up. We were loaded into boxcars for our trip to Wetzler. We arrived sometime in the afternoon. Once there we were given clothing to replace damaged articles. I was given shoes to replace my heated liners. (I wish I had kept them.) I retained my jacket but the heated liner had been removed. Each of us was given a parcel suitcase. This contained toilet articles, a sweater, pajamas, cigarettes, soap, and other sundry items.

At Wetzler we were quartered in tents according to rank. This was to be the separation point. Officers were sent to their camps and enlisted men were sent to theirs. The next day I was told to report to Lt. Gills, the American liaison officer. I was the ranking non-commissioned officer. Therefore I was to be in charge of the next group shipping out. I was told to sign a pledge that no one would escape. If anyone did I would be held responsible. I countered that I do not know what was in the minds of a thousand POWs. He said that the war was not going to last long and everyone before me had signed the pledge. We were going to Stalag Luft IV, an enlisted men's camp in Poland. Because we were going away from the American lines I thought the risk of attempted escape was low. So I signed the pledge and took the responsibility that went with it.

The next day we enlisted men shipped out. The walking wounded and sick were put in separate boxcars. They were attended to by GIs who had some first aid training. A German master sergeant was in charge of ine movement. *Being a POW train we had the lowest priority on the rails. Our train would be shunted to a side track when a higher priority train needed to pass. Whenever we stopped I had the master sergeant escort me so I could check on the condition of the men. I paid special attention to the sick and wounded.*

I remember at one stop a German troop train stopped along side us. Some of the soldiers got out and were walking around outside. Seeing us, one of them held up a newspaper. On the front page was a picture of a B-26 that had suffered a direct hit by flak and was a ball of fire. The German soldiers were laughing about it. The response by one of the men put the loss of one bomber out of thousands into perspective. He held up one forefinger and quizzically asked, "Ein" (one)? The sad part about this encounter was that these soldiers were so young, fourteen to sixteen years old. They were on their way to the Russian front. I wonder how many of them survived.

COMMENTARY

As the men were marched through the streets of Berlin the tension in the air was palpable. The jeering crowd had within their grasp a target to exact vengeance upon. But on that day the survivors of Crew 601 were fortunate. It was not uncommon for captured airmen to be beaten or killed by civilians bent on retaliation for the death and destruction caused by the bomber crews.

The Dulag Luft Interrogation Center in Frankfurt was the intelligence gathering site for the Luftwaffe. After three days in solitary confinement Dad went before the interrogator. The fact that the interrogator assumed Dad was in the 492nd Bomb Group was not surprising. When he was hauled out of the water his captors would have noted the type of aircraft. The tail markings identified which group it came from.

Dad notes that the liner to his heated flying suit was removed at the Dulag Luft. There was a good reason for this. The Germans confiscated the liner because they believed the POWs would use the heating wires for making radios.

His POW record is dated June 25, 1944, five days after he was shot down. It tells us more than name, rank, and service number. He is a Catholic and was born in Beloit, Wisconsin. His mother's maiden name is Debegnach and father's first name is Angelo. His wife is Mrs. Ethel Centore and her address is 13th Avenue in Dorothy, New Jersey. The number of children is listed as one, although that wouldn't happen until three months later. In civilian life he was a mechanic. There is only one entry that has any military significance. His "function" is listed as "Eng.". I was puzzled by the amount of information until I visited the Mighty Eighth Air Force Museum in Savannah, Georgia. There was, on display, a POW record of a navigator that had been shot down in October, 1943. He had listed all the same personal information as Dad's record.

The POW record lists physical characteristics and fingerprints. The first photo was taken shortly after he was shot down. (He is wearing his F-2 heated flying suit jacket.) The others were taken five days later at Dulag Luft. His height was 169 centimeters (5'7"). He weighed 65 kilograms (143 pounds).

. . .

The last flight record entry is "Closed Out M.I.A. 20June1944". (Author)

CHAPTER 19
PRISONER OF WAR 2494

After three or four days we reached the Gross Tychow station. We disembarked and trucks took the sick and wounded to the camp, Stalag Luft IV. The rest of us lined up in columns and took a leisurely walk through the woods to the camp. Arriving at the camp we were held in what was called a vorlager. We entered the building in groups. Once inside we were told to strip to bare flesh. We were searched, and that included every body cavity.

We stood in front of a line of tables. A guard went through our captive kits. My guard, who was later nicknamed "Washed-out Cadet," went through my property. He removed some of the articles and placed them on a shelf behind him. He ignored me when I asked why he was doing this. An interpreter was walking by and I asked him why this was happening. He said the items would be given to less fortunate POWs. I told him I was a better judge of who should get what. When he walked away I took matters into my own hands and went between the tables and began retrieving my things. Washed-out Cadet tried to stop me but I was determined. At the next table was a guard known as "Big Stoop." He had been given that nickname for his resemblance to a character from the comic strip "Terry and the Pirates." He took matters into his huge hands. He grabbed me and threw me across the room. I bounced off the wall, got up and staggered around. I was pretty dizzy and reached for the table to steady myself from falling again. The guard motioned to me to get back behind the table. He returned the items from my kit to the shelf. At this point I didn't care what he took.

We were then ordered to get dressed, get our things together, and go outside. They took a group of us to the area of the camp named Lager A. We were divided into groups of sixteen and assigned to different barracks. I went to Barracks 10 Room 4. I met my new roommates and got acquainted. Because I had been the leader of the contingent from Wetzler they appointed me the room leader. Before the week was out I was also appointed the Red Cross representative for Barracks 10. It was my job to distribute the Red Cross parcels when they came in. We were never given a complete parcel. They were opened by the Germans and broken down into smaller units. Cans of food were punctured so they had to be eaten soon after. This was to prevent prisoners from stockpiling supplies for an escape.

I would have some of my roommates help when the load was heavy. Everything would be laid out in our room and divided up. The other room leaders would take their share back to their roommates. I was also the canteen man and would pass out shaving gear and miscellaneous items. My next assignment was as the barracks librarian. What the heck I wasn't going anywhere. It gave me something to do and boredom was the biggest enemy.

COMMENTARY

The preceding was as far as Dad got in his writings of his time in as a POW. He would have added more, but unfortunately he passed away before he could finish it.

Robert Armstrong wrote about his POW experiences in "USA The Hard Way." Dad had an autographed copy. Armstrong signed it "for Nello Centore, a fellow kriegie." Dad would often use that strange term. The derivation of it turned out to be very simple. Americans have a habit of giving everything a nickname. The word kriegie is derived from kriegsgefangen, the German word for prisoner of war.

Most of this commentary was written from stories Dad told us about his three hundred plus days of captivity. Among other sources were some of Dad's roommates in Stalag Luft IV. 1983 Dad received audio tapes from Bob Johnson and Frank Dileva. They talked about their shared experiences in the camp. Frank also sent Dad a copy of a diary that was kept by fellow roommate Joe Fioretti. I decided to contact any of Dad's roommates I could find. I was sad to discover that 20 of the 27 men had passed away. That included Johnson, Dileva, and Fioretti. I couldn't find information on six others.

In 2009 I found one valid address and sent a letter of introduction. Within a week I received a call from Ken Garwood. He had been a B-17 radio operator in the 96th Bomb Group. Ken had been shot down not once, but twice! His crew flew its first mission on May 23, 1944. The target was the airfield at Chateaudun, France. When they reached the target anti-aircraft shells began exploding around them. Two of the four engines were shot up and failed. In an attempt to extend the range of their stricken craft, the gunners began throwing out ammunition, machine guns, and anything else to lighten the load. After crossing the French coast Radio Operator Garwood began sending out mayday calls. When a third engine failed the pilot knew he had to ditch the crippled plane in the English Channel. A British warship had heard the calls and arrived on the scene. All of the crewmembers survived and were returned to base.

On June 20, the same day Dad was shot down, the 96th Bomb Group hit the oil refinery at Magdeburg, Germany. After they released the bombs Garwood's plane was attacked by Focke-Wulf 190 fighters. With two engines on fire the pilot sounded the bail-out bell. All of Ken's crew with the exception of the flight engineer survived. The five surviving enlisted men were sent to Stalag Luft IV. Two of them, Ken Garwood and waist gunner William Blow became roommates of Dad's in Barracks 4.

After being processed at the transit camp, Dad was sent to Stalag Luft IV, a non-commissioned officers' camp. The feeling, and hope, that the war would be over by Christmas was commonly held after the D-Day invasion. That being the case, or at least the perception, there were no significant plans for escaping from Stalag Luft IV. On March 25, 1944 seventy six POWs escaped from Stalag Luft III, located in Sagan, in what is now Poland. The Steve McQueen movie, "The Great Escape," was based on the event. The results were not great as only three men made it to freedom. Hitler wanted the other seventy three shot but Hermann Goering intervened and got it reduced to fifty. The magnitude of the escape caused many changes to be made, both in how the camps were constructed and how escape attempts were punished. A poster was disseminated to all POW camps. It begins, "To all Prisoners of War! The escape from prison camps is no longer a sport!" It went on to blame the new policy on a "captured secret and confidential English military pamphlet" that called for every soldier to be a "potential gangster." The accusation would be comical if it weren't for the warning that those attempting to escape would be shot on sight. Dad remembers this new policy as being the result of a paranoid reaction to Operation Valkyrie, the unsuccessful July 20, 1944 plot to kill Hitler.

As you would expect, food was always on the kriegies' minds. Potato soup with turnip, with an occasional piece of horsemeat thrown in, and black bread was the standard meal. One man would go through the chow line and bring the meal back to his roommates.

Where that man positioned himself in the chow line was important. He would try to time his appearance in front of the cook as the soup was being ladled from the bottom of the pot. That way they got more stock than broth.

The kriegies received very little coal for the pot-bellied stove in the barracks. In their resourcefulness, they found there were boards on the ceiling of the building that could be fairly easily removed. They removed them and they burned them. Dad joked that he was surprised a strong wind never blew the roof off.

My brother Chip remembers Dad describing a very resourceful method they had to get more coal. Each barracks was issued a "ticket" that would be redeemed for a bucket of coal. The men told a guard that they would like to trade cigarettes for paper. The only stipulation was that the paper had to be a particular color. The guard got them the paper, which just happened to be the same color as the coal tickets. They cut the paper to the proper size. One of the men then painstakingly duplicated the print and made a series of bogus tickets which they successfully redeemed.

This was another example of the kriegies ongoing attempts to outsmart their captors. When Dad would tell these stories you got the impression it was a game of wits between them and the Germans. The object was survival but it also kept the men occupied during the long months of captivity. The inclination to always try to outsmart the system, to get something for nothing, was a trait Dad retained for the rest of his life. Whether he was buying a car, furniture, or dining out he was always had a reason why he should get a deal, a discount, or refund. Many people are good at bargaining, getting the most for their money. But Dad took it to another level. He seemed to enjoy this type of interaction as much for the sport of it as for any material gain.

Dad was always a stickler for cleanliness. He was assigned to a barracks that wasn't up to his standards. He organized a clean-up campaign. All but one of the men agreed to take part. For some reason, one man wouldn't put forth any effort. Dad confronted him. The disagreement escalated into an argument, then to a fist fight. Dad was a street fighter from the mean streets of New York City and prevailed. After seeing the results of their labor the Germans moved the men to different barracks and made that one the camp hospital.

That was always a point of pride for him. After this incident Dad was moved to Barracks 4, Room 4. This new location is displayed on both his POW record and the notice of my birth he received from the Red Cross in September.

We kids learned how much Dad believed in cleanliness. When the other kids were playing on Saturday morning, Dad had us cleaning the house. That, I suppose, was logical because we were the ones who messed it up. But he did take it to extremes. We had to use a toothbrush to clean the grout around the bathroom tile. If the dishes did not meet with his approval, all the dishes came out of the cabinets and were washed and dried. Only when our work passed his inspection were we allowed to go out.

Every day the camp had its new arrivals. A few weeks after Dad was shot down he saw an old friend being marched into Stalag Luft IV. It was his buddy John Crowley, the tail gunner on Lt. Frank Haag's Crew 611. John had been shot down on the costly Bernberg mission of July 7, 1944. John was from Cranston, Rhode Island. He and Dad had been together since basic training. Whenever they were transferred they always ended up in the same outfit. Now here they were, together again, this time behind barbed wire.

The Geneva Convention sets the rules for treatment of prisoners of war. One provision prohibits officers and non-commissioned officers from being forced to do manual labor. Because of this restriction time was heavy on the kriegies' hands. Charles Janis acknowledged this fact of life with the title of his book about his experiences in Stalag Luft IV. He chose to call it "Barbed Boredom." Incalculable miles were racked up walking the perimeter and talking. Dad described watching two German carpenters build a guard tower. All the work was done with hand tools only. What surprised Dad most was that no nails were used. The entire structure was held together with wooden pegs. Watching the construction was a pleasant diversion and the men were disappointed upon its completion.

A flight of four Luftwaffe fighters would regularly do aerobatics over the camp, showing off their mastery of the air. During one of these impromptu air shows one of the fighters crashed just outside the wire. The men cheered and cheered until the guards cut it short and made them return to their barracks.

The German guards were typically older men than those on the front lines. Many were brutal and were reported for war crimes at war's end. However, there were instances when they did show their humanity. More than once a guard proudly showed Dad pictures of his "Frau und Kinder," his wife and children. Dad said that although he hated his German captors he felt sorry for them. He was going home to a beautiful country, untouched by war. They on the other hand were going home to a devastated land and populace.

Dad wasn't alone in his hatred of "Big Stoop." His real name was Sergeant Hans Schmidt. He was six foot seven and weighed over 300 pounds. Even the other guards were afraid of him. There were rumors that he was a member of the Gestapo. He was by all accounts a sadist who enjoyed physically abusing his charges. One of his painful signature moves was boxing a prisoner's ears with his huge ham hands. In some cases ruptured eardrums were the result. After their liberation the kriegies were debriefed and asked about any war crimes they may have witnessed. When Dad brought up the name Big Stoop to the inquiring officer, he replied, "I knew you were going to say that. Everyone gives us that name." There is an account by S/Sgt Robert Scalley that justice was meted out to Big Stoop. After General Patton liberated the POW camp at Mooseburg, Scalley and a couple of friends were returning from town after dark. They came upon a body, a large body, a large headless body. Scalley said of their gruesome discovery, "I'm almost certain it was Big Stoop."

In January of 1945 the Russian Army was advancing through Poland and closing in on the non-commissioned officers' camp Stalag Luft IV. The order came down from the German High Command to evacuate the camp. The camp's population had grown to over 9,000 men. On January 28th Dad and John Crowley were in a group of 3,000 who left the camp by train, destination unknown.

In an article published in The Ex-POW Bulletin, Richard Bing described the train ride. Most of the men on the train were the sick and wounded. How the rest of the train contingent was chosen is unclear. As they left for the train Bing and the others felt guilty leaving their buddies behind.

When they got to the railway station the men were stuffed into filthy cattle cars, sixty in each one. There was little open space. The men had to take turns lying down on the cold floor. The latrine was a bucket hanging on a nail. Former POW Roy Shenkel remembers not being given any food and little water. What water they did get gave many of them diarrhea, which only compounded the misery. One of the men in Shenkel's cattle car died in transit.

When the train stopped in Stettin, Germany a riot broke out as German civilians attempted to take over the train. They wanted to escape the advancing Russian Army and thought they should be given priority over the prisoners. The guards fired their weapons and restored order. A short time later, Royal Air Force bombers began bombing the rail yard. The POWs suffered no casualties in the attack and their journey continued.

As absurd as it sounds, the men who left Stalag Luft IV by train were lucky by comparison. The remaining 6,000 left the camp on what became known as the "Black March." They were marched out in groups of 250 to 300. Between February 6th and May 2nd they trod over 600 miles over frozen ground and suffered indescribable privation. On April 19, 1945, sixty men were killed by RAF fighters who mistook the column for German troops. Possibly as many as 1,300 men were lost to disease, starvation, and exposure.

Most of the men from Room 4 went on the march. Joe Fioretti, of the 91st Bomb Group, kept a diary. The diary begins in November 1944, five months after he was shot down. The entries for the time on the march tell of starvation, exposure, and cruelty. After reading the diary, Ken Garwood said that as bad as Fioretti's words portrayed the march, the experience was far worse. If they were lucky, the men were herded into a barn to spend the night. But on most nights they slept outside, in the cold rain and snow.

Those that left the camp by train were, with few exceptions, locked in the cattle cars for eight days. Finally, on February 7, 1945, they pulled into the station at Barth, Germany. They were taken to Stalag Luft I, an officers' camp. Colonel Hubert Zemke was the ranking American POW. Zemke had commanded the famous 56th Fighter Group. Under his leadership the group had shot down 500 German aircraft. He was transferred to the 479th Fighter Group trading in his P-47 Thunderbolt for a P-51 Mustang. In October 1944 he wanted to lead one more mission before taking, against his will, a staff position at 8th Air Force headquarters. Flying through a violent storm over enemy territory a wing was sheared off his Mustang. Rather than "flying a desk" in England Zemke spent the rest of the war as a prisoner of war.

Another member of "Zemke's Wolfpack," as the 56th FG was known, was Lt. Col. Francis Gabreski. On April 12, 1945 President Roosevelt died in Warm Springs, Georgia. American men and women in uniform marked the passing of their Commander-in Chief. American prisoners of war were no different. At Stalag Luft I a formation of enlisted men was held with Gabreski leading the memorial service. At one point in the ceremony, Gabreski wanted to move the formation. He gave the men the preparatory command, "Forward." Finding it difficult not to anticipate the command, the men leaned forward, fully expecting to hear the word "March." Gabreski evidently changed his mind and instead gave the command "Present arms." The formation stumbled forward, stepped back, and snapped a hand salute. The German guards watching the assembly started laughing at their charges. After the ceremony Gabreski chewed out the men, telling them he wouldn't "want them in his Boy Scout troop". Dad always gave Gabreski his due however, calling him an outstanding fighter pilot. Gabby had shot down 28 German aircraft before the mission that landed him in kriegie camp. Even then he hadn't been shot down. During a strafing run on a German airfield, he flew so low that the propeller on his P-47 Thunderbolt struck the ground and he crashed landed. During the Korean War he was credited with shooting down 6.5 MIG fighters, making him one of the few fighter pilots to become an ace in two wars.

Stalag Luft I was liberated by the Russian Army on May 1, 1945. The first thing the men did was to tear down the fences. Although Dad chose not to, some of the men went to the neighboring town of Barth. One of them told him he and his buddy saw one of the German guards on the street wearing civilian clothes. The men summoned two Russian soldiers and pointed out their former captor as a "soldat" and he was taken away. Former POW Robert Armstrong describes the incident as he actually witnessed it. Ten POWs were walking together on a street in Barth. The enlisted men realized that a man coming toward them in civilian clothes was a guard from Stalag Luft IV they had nicknamed "Hollywood." The officer in charge of the group, a captain, told everyone to remain there until he came back. He went to the Russian headquarters, which they had just passed, and returned with three Russian soldiers. They took Hollywood away. Armstrong asked the captain what would happen to him. The captain replied that they may have just sentenced the man to death. He was to be taken to the train station and sent to Russia. They admitted to themselves that Hollywood was an obnoxious person, but he never harmed anyone. The former captives were shaken as the reality of the situation sank in. There was silence for the next twenty minutes as they forced the thought of Hollywood's bleak future from their minds.

When the camp was liberated, Colonel Zemke had the German POW records given to the men as mementos of their ordeal. We still have the record and the jacket Dad wore in prison camp.

After the D-Day landings nine camps were established in the vicinity of Le Harve, France. They were called "cigarette camps," each being named for a popular brand of smokes. Their original purpose was to process the thousands of combat troops arriving in France prior to their going into battle. After V-E (Victory in Europe) Day they became processing centers for the men's return to the States. These camps were also repatriation centers for American POWs held by the Germans. Dad was sent to Camp Lucky Strike located in Saint-Sylvian, France. General, and later President, Dwight D. Eisenhower, described an incident at Camp Lucky Strike that Dad was a witness to. Ike had spoken before many groups of men but was at a loss for words as he stood before the emaciated former POWs. Then he had what he called "a happy thought." He gave the men a choice. They could sail home on ships loaded at the normal capacity, one man per bunk. But if they chose to, they could double up and share the bunks twelve hours on, twelve hours off. That way they could get them home twice as quickly. The roar of the crowd left no doubt that they wanted to get home as soon as possible. However, he would abide by their decision, but there was one thing Ike insisted on. He did not want to hear of anyone writing to their congressmen to complain about overcrowded conditions. In the end, not one complaint was received. By war's end, over three million men were processed through the "cigarette camps."

Dad talked about his time in prison camp, not to brag about how much he endured, although he had every right to, but to teach us that you can survive anything if you don't give up hope and keep pushing yourself. He said, "I wouldn't do it over again for a million dollars, but it was a million dollar experience". Ken Garwood voiced a similar sentiment. He said, "I wouldn't give up a minute I spent in prison camp. It was an experience. I came through it and I never regretted it".

• • •

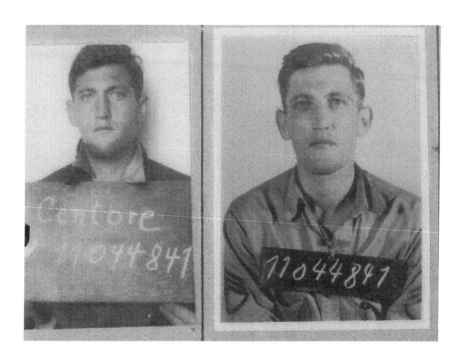

POW photographs of Nello, the first taken shortly after being captured, and the second six days later. (Author)

CHAPTER 20
RETURNING HOME

It was late at night when I took a cab from Vineland to Dorothy, New Jersey. As the driver proceeded down 13th Avenue, we drove into the wrong driveway. I got out of the cab and was greeted by the next door neighbors, Agnes and Martin. I paid the driver and said I would walk to Ethel's house. It was a dark night and I was lucky not to break my neck walking through the field between the houses. The house was dark when I knocked on the door. The lights came on and my father-in-law greeted me and the excitement started. Ethel and her mother came out. Kisses, hugs, and tears were shared by all. After this settled down Ethel took me into the bedroom to show me my son who was sleeping soundly. She wanted to pick him up for me to hold him but I said to let him sleep. I didn't want to break his sleep cycle but I really wanted to hold him. But I figured I would get to hold him for many years to come. We stayed up for a couple of hours drinking schnapps and coffee. I think I must have started dozing. It had been a long day. I was home at last. No more German guards telling me what to do. I had a wife that would do that from now on!

COMMENTARY

This must have been a wonderful homecoming. At this point Mom and Dad had been married for less than two years but had not seen each other in a year and a half.

I was nine months old when Dad came home and I had gotten quite used to the status quo. My mother and my grandmother doted on me. I always got my way and would hold my breath until I turned blue if I wasn't receiving the attention I felt I deserved. But Dad quickly put a stop to that. If I wanted to hold my breath, fine, go ahead. He forbade my grandmother to rush over to pick me up and walk me around the room. I had indeed met my match. The party was over.

• • •

Rick, Ethel, and Nello in 1945. (J. Dorsey)

CHAPTER 21
LADY IN WAITING

The following essay was written by my mother for a college writing course. I was thrilled to find it among my Dad's personal effects. Her words convey so well what she went through during those trying times.

Our courtship, constantly being interrupted by whoever was trying to keep a war going, was like a long string of Chinese firecrackers. There were so few days for us to spend together, and so much time to wait between, that we filled every moment with things to do, places to go.

Walking the streets of New York was our favorite. Fifth Avenue with its tantalizing windows at two in the morning, held a stillness that belonged only to us.

Saying good-bye each time, at Penn Station, always left a leaden hollowness within that would linger until a letter arrived. Inevitably, one of the visits would be the last in a long time, or at worst, forever. He must have felt this too for, on the first day of a ten-day furlough, he suggested we marry the next day (we had been engaged for two months). The three days that followed were a mad frenzy of blood tests, shopping and trying to find someone willing to marry us. Nobody could or wanted to—I was too young and we were of different faiths. We were finally married by the priest who had first refused us. Our wedding day in September was as hectic as our courtship had been; beginning with a long train ride to fetch my parents, a late afternoon ceremony in the rectory and a reception at a restaurant chosen later. It was a small Italian place with lots of latticework and fake grapes hanging everywhere. The most elaborate plans could not have produced a happier wedding.

Our four-day honeymoon was shortened to two days by a crisp telegram calling him back to do absolutely nothing for a month. We made up for it two months later when he was sent to Florida. His mother shooed me off to spend ten glorious days with him. Enduring four days of soot and bad food, on a train packed with weary wives, soldiers and crying children; sometimes sitting on a suitcase, even holding a baby in order to gain a seat, I gave no thought to the inconvenience.

When I returned, I wondered if I would see him again. On Christmas morning I awakened to find him bending over to kiss me. Joy-filled days followed that were to be our last together for a long time. On Easter Sunday, he was flying to England, knowing happily that our first child was to be born on my birthday in September.

I returned to my father's farm and kept myself occupied with chores at a leisurely pace, leaving behind the non-stop madness of city living that dehumanizes everyone caught up in it.

The peace I felt did not last. In June, my bothers took me riding to tell me that my husband was missing over Germany. I felt desolate but always thought the worst would never happen as youth is apt to do. After two months came the joyful word that he had been captured and was well.

Three days after my birthday, during the night, I awoke, aware that this was it. A hurricane was raging outside. Tree branches were beating a mad tattoo on our roof. I lay in bed quietly, feeling no real hurry. Right after dawn, the storm abated; I called to my father who walked a mile to the post office (we had no phone, no car) to tell my friend who had offered to take me to the hospital.

The ride was marked by detours and stops where tree limbs stretched across the road. It was comforting to place myself in the capable hands of the doctors and nurses. That evening our first son, Ricky, was born. Two days later I was overjoyed to receive a single folded sheet marked "Kriegsgefangenen" (prisoner-of-war), written by him, wishing us well. It was to be two more months before he learned that he had become a father. Eleven months after he had been shot down, Ricky and I welcomed him home. Our married life had truly begun.

Ethel Centore October 24, 1972

• • •

Ethel and Nello on their wedding day in 1943. (J. Dorsey)

CHAPTER 22
THE FATE OF THE 492ND
BOMB GROUP

In the summer of 1944 the Eighth Air Force was undertaking a reorganization of its three heavy bombardment divisions. The First Division flew Boeing B-17 Flying Fortresses. The Second Division, which included the 492nd Bomb Group, flew Consolidated B-24 Liberators. The Third Division flew both types of heavy bombers. Because of optimal speed and altitude differences, the two types did not work well together. There was a preference within the Eighth Air Force for the B-17. Had the war in Europe continued, the eventual aim was to equip the entire Eighth Air Force with Boeing bombers. But in the short term the goal was to make the Third Division an entirely B-17 force. To accomplish that, four groups traded in their B-24s and received B-17s.

Within that reorganization the decision was made to eliminate one B-24 group. The loss of 55 aircraft and crews in 67 missions sealed the fate of the 492nd. Analyzing the operational history of the group you see that the majority of those losses were suffered on just three missions.

The first of these missions took place a week after the group started flying combat. On May 19th the group flew Mission 5. The target was Brunswick, Germany. After reaching the initial point the group turned toward the target. A force of 40 German fighters attacked. The group was without fighter protection and eight aircraft were shot down. The 492nd had its first combat losses, 43 men killed and 34 captured.

The second of the three worst missions was the June 20th mission to Politz. The 492nd dispatched 35 bombers. On Mission 34 the group suffered its highest one-day losses. As the group made a right turn to the initial point for the run to the target the low left section swung away from the lead and high right sections. This couldn't have happened at a worst time as the allied fighter escort was absent. They were pounced upon by German ace Rudy Desseau's bomber destroyer group, ZG 26. The Germans decimated the low left section with rockets, cannon, and machine gun fire. Only one crew from that section returned to North Pickenham. Nine went down in a matter of minutes. Five others were able to make it to Sweden. The final tally was 14 aircraft lost, with 77 men killed in action, 22 taken prisoner, and 40 interned in Sweden. Two of the prisoners of war died in captivity.

The third of these costly missions was Mission 46 to Bernberg, Germany. This time is was the 859th Bomb Squadron who would take the hardest hit. The group could only muster 23 aircraft in two sections and a squadron from the 392nd Bomb Group filled out the three section attacking force. As they approached the target they found themselves on a collision course with a Liberator that was returning after bombing another target. Some groups changed course and others didn't. The 492nd maintained course and in the confusion was without fighter protection. The Luftwaffe hit them and hit them hard. Twelve aircraft went down with 67 men killed and 52 taken prisoner.

These three missions comprised only five percent of the total number flown by the group. But they accounted for over 60 percent of the losses in men and aircraft. The 492nd Bomb Group was disbanded on August 7, 1944, after 89 days of combat. Its remaining aircraft and crews were reassigned to other groups in the Second Air Division.

There has always been a question as to why the 492nd suffered such high losses. Theories abound. Some say their formations were too tight; others say too loose. One theory is that in being equipped with a majority of unpainted aircraft, the group's silver airplanes were easily singled out for destruction by German fighters. This theory appears to be based on the idea that the group's losses were disproportionately due to enemy fighters rather than antiaircraft fire. But in the end the title of Allan Blue's excellent history of the 492nd may state it best. It was simply the "Fortunes of War."

• • •

492nd Bomb Group Veterans at the 2008 reunion in Minneapolis. (Author)

EPILOGUE

It has been over sixty years since the 492nd Bomb Group took to the war to the German heartland. Many of those heroic men are gone now. Some were lost in the cold skies over Europe. We see them in the crew photographs, shoulder to shoulder in front of silver or olive drab Liberators. They look out at us, 20 years old forever.

After the war was over the veterans of the 492nd returned home and went their separate ways. They pursued careers and raised families. Contacting members of the group and their families has been one of the most rewarding aspects of this research.

Pete Val Preda returned to Rutland, Vermont, after the war. He started a very successful automobile dealership, Val Preda Olds Cadillac. Everyone knows of the good work done at the children's hospitals operated by the Shriners International. Pete was a past Imperial Potentate of that fine organization. He passed away on August 14, 1995. His daughter Diana, whose name would have been painted on her Dad's airplane if it had survived, lives in Vermont.

Rudie Bartel was one of the two navigators on Crew 601 for the Politz mission. Some of the information about the final mission was gleaned from a poignant letter he wrote to Douglas Pierce's mother after the war. Rudie retired as a major in the U.S. Air Force. He passed away on March 9, 2005.

Elvern Seitzinger, the original co-pilot of Crew 601, passed away on July 24, 2006.

Luke Rybarczyk, the original bombardier of Crew 601, had been reassigned to Crew 608. The entire crew was lost on the June 20 Politz mission. He is remembered on the Wall of the Missing in Cambridge, England.

Norman Burns, the original navigator of Crew 601, was reassigned to Crew 606. On July 3, 1944, he was transferred to the 44th Bomb Group.

Jack Reed is buried in the Ardennes American Cemetery in Neupre, Belgium. I shared that information with Jack's niece and nephew. They were surprised to learn that their uncle's body had been recovered. Jack's parents went to their graves believing his remains were never found.

Arthur St. Pierre's remains were returned to the United States for burial. His wife Yvette and my mother rode the train together to visit their husbands in Florida in October, 1943. Yvette and Arthur had no children. A memorial plaque in his honor is located at the corner of South Maple Street and South Willow Street in Manchester, New Hampshire.

Miles Toepper's remains were returned for burial in the United States. He was bumped off the airplane for the flight to England by Lt. Lofdahl. He went overseas by ship and joined the crew in North Pickenham. Because of this he is not in the official crew photograph. Miles was from Forest Park, Illinois.

Douglas Pierce was reported to have been buried on Rugen Island in Germany. But the location of his final resting place has been lost forever. His name is in on the Wall of the Missing in Cambridge, England. His nephew Lynn contacted Dad for information on his uncle. Dad wrote the story of their final mission in response.

Walter Kean settled in Derby, Connecticut, after the war. I remember a family visit to his home when I was a youngster. My sister Judy and I were shocked to see him push a pencil right through his ankle! Of course, we didn't know at the time he had a prosthetic leg.

My Dad, Nello Centore, took advantage of the GI Bill and returned to school. He became a licensed aircraft mechanic. In 1982 he retired from the Kaman Corporation as a general foreman after a 30-year career. He and my Mom Ethel had three more children, daughter Judy and sons Chip and Tom. Mom was killed in an automobile accident in 1975. Dad married Jean Sayles in 1982. Pete and Charlotte Val Preda attended the wedding. He passed away on October 11, 2007.

John Crowley, whose service history parallels my Dad's, returned to his home state of Rhode Island after the war. He joined the Providence Police Department and retired after a long career. John passed away in 1995. His daughter Ann lives in Massachusetts. She shared with me that Arthur St. Pierre was the best man at her Mom and Dad's wedding in December. Dad probably would have been the best man but he was on leave with my Mom at the time. That was lucky for me as I was born the following September.

Herschel Smith's aircraft received severe battle damage on a mission to Munich, Germany. He landed his crippled craft in Ghedi, Italy. The crew was captured and sent to various prisoner of war camps.

Herschel went to Stalag Luft I, the same camp Dad was sent to after Stalag Luft IV was closed. After the war, Herschel returned home to Germantown, Ohio where he retired from the U. S. Postal Service.

It has been my privilege to meet many of the men of the 492nd at the group's annual reunions. Many of them flew the Politz mission with my Dad. Bob Cash was the radio operator on the McKoy crew in the "Ruptured Duck." Milton Goodridge was the pilot of "Bottle Baby." Both men were the sole survivors of their crews.

Bill Beasley was the tail gunner on the Harris crew. They were flying in the "Silver Witch" on the same Politz mission Dad was shot down on. The battle damage they received made it impossible to return to England and they made a successful landing in Sweden. He and his wife Norma established the tradition of the annual reunion of the 492nd Bomb Group. Bill passed away on February 22, 2009.

Howard Heckmann was the ball turret gunner on the Lewis crew. Their Liberator, named "Uninvited," was shot down on the Brunswick mission. He was sent to Stalag Luft IV. Howard took advantage of the GI Bill after the war and became a successful architect. He is also the very entertaining host of the reunion raffles.

Ernie Haar was the pilot of the 859th Bomb Squadron's "Umbriago." I'll always remember one particular evening in the lounge at the 2008 reunion in Minneapolis. A dozen of us sat around over drinks as Ernie held court and regaled us with his many stories.

Charles Arnett was the pilot of "Boomerang." He was shot down on the Brunswick mission and was sent to Stalag Luft III. We are all in his debt for making it possible for his sons David and Paul to develop the 492nd Bomb Group website. Charles passed away on March 12, 2008.

Bob Scott was the pilot of one of only six crews to fly thirty missions with the group. Bob and his family make up one of the larger contingents at the group's reunions.

George Worthington's damaged aircraft made it to Sweden on the first Politz mission. His descriptions of being interned in that neutral country stand in stark contrast to the treatment of those who became prisoners of the Germans.

I have also met many other sons and daughters of 492nd vets. This book is dedicated to four of them. Kathy Jensen is the daughter of Laurence Nursall. He was the radio operator on the Herbert crew (802). He was lost on the Brunswick mission, May 19, 1944. Billy Johnson is the daughter of William Sheely. Bill was the tail gunner on the Smiley crew (910). He was lost on the Bernberg mission, July 7, 1944. Judith Larrivee O'Connor is the daughter of Francis Larrivee. Francis was also lost on the Bernberg mission. He was a waist gunner on the McMurray crew (801). Patrick Byrne is the son of Austin Byrne. Austin was the Operations Officer of the 857th Bomb Squadron. He was lost on the next to the last mission of the group to Hamburg, Germany, on August 6, 1944. Kathy, Billy, Judith, and Pat attend the reunions in their fathers' memory. It is an honor for me to call these "Gold Star Kids" my friends.

• • •

Jean and Nello Centore

BIBLIOGRAPHY

Armstrong, Roger W. *USA The Hard Way*. Orange County, California: Quail House Publishing, 1991

Arnett, David & Arnett Paul. *The 492nd Bomb Group Website*, Mesa, Arizona: www.492ndbombgroup.com, 2009

Bailey, Mike & North, Tony. *Liberator Album*. Norfolk, England: Tony North, 1981

Bastein, Charles. *32 Co-pilots*. Victoria, B.C., Canada: Trafford Publishing, 2004

Birdsall, Steve. *The B-24 Liberator*. ARCO Publishing Company, 1968

Birdsall, Steve. *Log of the Liberators*. Garden City, New York: Doubleday, 1973

Blue, Allan G. *Fortunes of War*. Fallbrook, California: Aero Publishers, 1967

Blue, Allan G. *The B-24 Liberator*. Surrey, England: Ian Allan Ltd, 1976

Bodle, Peter. *The 492nd and 491st Bomb Groups in Norfolk*. Norfolk, England: Liberator Publishing, 2006

Bowman, Martin. *Fields of Little America*. Norwich, England: Wensum Books, 1977

Bowman, Martin. *The B-24 Liberator 1939-1945*. Norwich, England: Wensum Books, 1979

Consolidated Aircraft, *Flight Manual for B-24 Liberator*. Appleton, Wisconsin: Aviation Publications, 1977

De Seversky, Alexander P. *Victory through Air Power*. New York, New York: Simon and Schuster, 1942

Dorr, Robert F. *B-24 Liberator Units of the Eighth Air Force*. Oxford, England: Osprey Publishing, 1999

Eisenhower, Dwight D. *Crusade in Europe*. New York, New York: Doubleday, 1948

Fioretti, Joseph Jr. *A Wartime Log*. Geneva, Switzerland: The War Prisoners' Aid of the YMCA, 1945

Freeman, Roger & Zemke, Hubert. *Zemke's Stalag*. Washington, DC: Smithsonian Institution Press, 1991

Hatton, Greg. *Stories My Father Never Told Me.* Brooklyn, New York: Greg Hatton, 1993

Ives, Russell. *89 Days.* Huddersfield, United Kingdom: Kall Kwik Printing, 1998

Janis, Charles. *Barbed Boredom.* Irvington, New Jersey: Charles Janis, 1950

Jones, Lloyd S. *U.S. Bombers.* Fallbrook, California: Aero Publishers, Inc., 1962

Klinkowitz, Jerome. *Yanks over Europe.* Lexington, Kentucky: The University Press of Kentucky, 1996

Laird, Robert E. *Coming Home on Three.* Rutland, Vermont: Sharp and Company Printers, 2006

Mahoney, James J. & Brian H. *Reluctant Witness.* Victoria, B.C., Canada: Trafford Publishing, 2001

Martin, Adrian R. & Stephenson, Larry W. *Operation Plum.* College Station, Texas: Texas A & M University Press, 2008

Maurer, Maurer. *Air Force Combat Units of World War II.* Edison, New Jersey: Chartwell Books, 1961

Nichol, John & Rennell, Tony. *The Last Escape.* New York, New York: Penguin Group, 2002

Punka, George. *Messerschmitt Me 210/410 in action.* Carrollton, Texas: Squadron/Signal Publications, 1994

Simmons, Kenneth W. *Prisoner of War.* New York, New York: Bantam Books, 1988

Speer, Albert. *Inside the Third Reich.* New York, New York: Galahad Books, 1970

• • •

4710171R0

Made in the USA
Charleston, SC
05 March 2010